CONFLICT RESOLUTION QUARTERLY

Editorial Board Members

Conflict Resolution Quarterly (ISSN 1536-5581) is published quarterly by Wiley Subscription Services, Inc., A Wiley company, at Jossey-Bass and the Association for Conflict Resolution. A subscription is included as a benefit of membership. For information about becoming a member of the Association for Conflict Resolution, please contact ACR's membership department at (202) 464-9700, or visit www.acresolution.org.

Conflict Resolution Quarterly is indexed in PsycINFO, Sociological Abstracts, the National Child Support Enforcement Clearinghouse, and the International Bibliography of the Social Sciences.

TO ORDER subscriptions or single issues, please refer to the Ordering Information page at the back of this issue.

EDITORIAL CORRESPONDENCE: see the Information for Contributors pages at the back of this issue.

www.josseybass.com

CONTENTS

EDITOR'S INTRODUCTION

Over the past month, as I finalized the contents of this issue, I have had the opportunity to participate in several meetings concerning conflict resolution education and the future policy and research agendas for this portion of our field. I have been heartened by the consensus of support for CRE and reinforced in my belief that one of the major contributions of *Conflict Resolution Quarterly* is to promote and report research on the efficacy of CRE and related efforts. I have been alarmed by the sense of urgency and the evaporating opportunity to share "research proven practices" with the educational community in a timely manner so they can use this information to secure rapidly dwindling resources from the federal government. I have been comforted by the new and renewed commitment to partnership among major organizations in the field, "walking their talk" of collaboration with each other rather than competing against the other. I have also been profoundly saddened by the challenge to several institutions that have been leaders in this field. Mostly, I have been emboldened to assertively pursue what I perceive to be the most important next step for conflict resolution education: the development of preservice education initiatives for elementary and secondary school teachers in conjunction with mentoring structures supported by solid in-service work.

Although it is highly unusual, and certainly precedent-setting in my editorship, I would like to dedicate this issue to Jennifer Batton, director of the schools programs at the Ohio Commission for Dispute Resolution and Conflict Management. This past year, faced with serious financial shortfalls, the Ohio legislature proposed cutting the commission's funding. As June proceeds quickly to a close, it appears that all efforts (some of which were almost heroic) to save the school programs of the commission and get funding restored by the legislature have failed. With this decision, Ohio and the nation have lost the leading CRE state institution in the country.

Established by the Ohio legislature in 1989, the commission provided dispute resolution programs and services throughout the state, working with schools, courts, communities, and state and local government. Since the early 1990s, the commission and the Ohio Department of Education worked together to furnish the financial and administrative support necessary to promote conflict resolution education in primary and secondary public schools. Each school year, the commission and ODE awarded competitive grants to Ohio's K–12 public schools to design, implement, and evaluate conflict resolution programs. Since 1994, more than seven hundred conflict resolution grants have been awarded. In addition to the grant awards, the commission and ODE make available training, technical assistance, and age-appropriate lesson plans and resource materials to grantee schools. Teachers, staff, and administrators are trained in how to integrate conflict resolution as a life skill into existing curricula and how to facilitate positive change within school communities by aligning mission statements, disciplinary procedures, and team building efforts with conflict resolution concepts and theories. Today more than fourteen hundred public schools in more than 380 of Ohio's 612 school districts report having a conflict resolution program in place. The commission led the way in the development of the Higher Education Institute, to bring higher education faculty together to find ways to work CRE into preservice curricula.

Jennifer Batton has been the fire, insight, and energy behind this awesome initiative. As her many admirers will concur, Jennifer is committed to thoughtful programming, institutionalization, and evaluation of conflict resolution education. For almost a decade, she has made the Ohio Commission for Dispute Resolution and Conflict Management the most innovative and respected agency in CRE. A friend recently sent me a wonderful quote from Thomas Edison: "If we all did the things we are capable of doing, we would literally astound ourselves." It's hard to imagine anyone doing more than Jennifer Batton has done for CRE, and hard to imagine anyone in witness who has not been astounded by her accomplishments. Hopefully, Jennifer will have the chance to continue to inspire CRE educators and professionals, among them the contributors to this volume.

There is no doubt that the name of the game is research-proven practices. Under the No Child Left Behind Act, funding for conflict education and social and emotional learning comes largely from Safe and Drug Free schools money, which requires funding only for programs or practices that have been proven effective through quality evaluation research. Thus it is imperative that there be outlets for publishing research in this area. There are far too few.

It is also important that emphasis be given to research that addresses the unanswered questions about CRE. The pieces selected for this issue speak to critical but underresearched areas of conflict resolution education.

Nancy Burrell, Cindy Zirbel, and Mike Allen present a sophisticated meta-analysis of peer mediation research. Peer mediation has long been the most common and most recognized form of conflict resolution education. Unfortunately, in recent years it has been challenged as ineffective, largely because of the conclusions printed in the recent surgeon general's report on youth violence prevention (*Youth Violence,* 2001). The report quotes Gottfredson's (1997) conclusion that peer mediation programs are ineffective and may even be counterproductive. This blanket conclusion has been used to argue against funding for these programs. Careful reading of the Preface to the surgeon general's report finds a clarification that "effectiveness" in this analysis means reduction or prevention of serious physical aggression and assault. Thus peer mediation programs, which were never designed to prevent serious physical violence but were intended to teach constructive life skills with disciplinary benefit to schools, were painted with far too broad a brush. Many researchers have known and argued that peer mediation programs are quite effective in a variety of ways. This meta-analysis helps us appreciate the body of research on this important conflict resolution education form.

A common critique of CRE and social and emotional learning (SEL) efforts is that they may teach skills but have little impact on more fundamental orientations to social interaction. To put it simply, they might teach students how to behave appropriately but do little to encourage them to want to behave appropriately. Warren Heydenberk, Roberta Heydenberk, and Sharon Perkins Bailey have made a great contribution to the literature in the five-year study of the impact of conflict education on children's moral reasoning. They lay a compelling framework for the importance of moral reasoning as a cornerstone of social and emotional competence. They detail the research that links moral reasoning with a host of positive outcomes. Their study of the effects of a comprehensive conflict resolution program, Project Peace, was conducted in urban and suburban schools in the Philadelphia area and proves that CRE does increase moral reasoning.

Some of us who have worked in the field for more than a decade are witnessing the second generation of students initially educated in CRE coming into colleges and universities. It is always amazing that time has passed this quickly, and exciting to contemplate the long-term impact of these programs. As the field matures, there comes a corresponding interest in examining how K–college educational initiatives can be better coordinated to maximize capacity and learning processes. Pamela Lane-Garon and Tim Richardson report on Mediator Mentors, a project involving university students trained in CRE mentoring elementary school students. They tell of the specific experience of the Herndon-Barstow elementary school in California. The CRE program resulted in improved cognitive and affective perspective taking by peer mediators and an improved school climate.

One challenge in researching CRE is finding measures that are context-relevant and age-appropriate for students. Too often researchers are trying to use instruments developed for adult populations to assess children. William Kimsey and Rex Fuller decided that, given the reliance on conflict styles as an "outcome of interest," it behooved them to develop a message-based conflict styles measure that was tailored for use in K–12 populations. Their article reports on the development and validation of that measure.

This September, the European Center for Violence Prevention will host an international conference on conflict resolution education. This timely event reminds us that there's a big world out there and a number of critical CRE initiatives that we need to know about. It is in this spirit that I was particularly pleased to have Lisa Shochat's piece on the *Nashe Maalo* project of Search for Common Ground in Macedonia. This project is compelling and unique for several reasons. First, it concerns conflict education pro-gramming outside of schools. In general, we are too reliant on traditional K–12 educational institutions as the delivery mechanism for conflict education. The *Nashe Maalo* project reminds us that there are a plethora of media available for learning in a diverse set of life contexts. Second, this project concerns conflict education in a conflict-ridden society where interethnic conflict and its negative manifestations have reached alarming proportions, with devastating social costs. Perhaps because the social con-dition is so dire, the research reports of positive impact carry more weight. It's nice when something works, but wonderful if it works when it's most needed.

It is equally important to realize that there are diverse populations in the United States, as well as around the world, in need of conflict education. Yet this is most definitely not a one-size-fits all endeavor. Too often, we see efforts that assume similarity in views of conflict and conflict management instead of asking whether that assumption is warranted. Michelle Scott argues that, as a field, we need to spend more energy on understanding assumptions about conflict in diverse populations. Her qualitative study of intragroup conflict behavior among African American inner-city youth reveal a unique orientation these students have about conflict. She suggests several insights from the research that can be used in the design and delivery of conflict education programs targeted for these students.

Rebecca Sanford and I contribute the last article to this issue. We report on one of the sites in the National Curriculum Integration Project, designed to deliver conflict education through ongoing curricula (language arts, math, science) in middle schools. The research was primarily interested in how conflict education affected the development of caring communities in the classroom. Happily, the research revealed that CRE has a significant and lasting impact on students' perceptions of a physically, emotionally, and psychologically safe learning environment.

Once again, this issue presents a segment of Research Matters. In this case, the research reported briefly by Jennifer Batton concerns cost-benefit analysis conducted by Ray Hart of Kent State University. In the ADR field, we know that cost effectiveness has been an important outcome for administrators. Does mediation cost less than court? School administrators concerned about the bottom line will find Hart's comparative analyses of formal disciplinary action versus mediation and CRE informative. The CRE approaches not only yield the positive personal and social benefits discussed in the rest of this issue but also cost far less than more punitive disciplinary structures.

TRICIA S. JONES
Editor-in-Chief

References

Gottfredson, D. C. "School-Based Crime Prevention." In L. W. Sherman, D. C. Gottfredson, D. Mackenzie, J. Eck, P. Reuter, and S. Bushway (eds.), *Preventing Crime: What Works, What Doesn't, What's Promising. A Report to the United States Congress.* (NCJ 171676). Washington, D.C.: U.S. Department of Justice, Office of Justice Programs, 1997.

Youth Violence: A Report of the Surgeon General. Washington, D.C.: Department of Health and Human Services, 2001.

Evaluating Peer Mediation Outcomes in Educational Settings: A Meta-Analytic Review

NANCY A. BURRELL

CINDY S. ZIRBEL

MIKE ALLEN

This investigation summarizes existing research on peer mediation outcomes in school-based settings. The meta-analytic review examines the outcomes associated with incorporating a mediation program to manage school conflict. Results indicate a 93 percent agreement rate and that 88 percent of the participants were satisfied with the agreements reached. The review answers critics and demonstrates the value of school-based mediation programs.

The national focus for educators seems to be on increasing reading and math test scores rather than on curriculum-based conflict resolution programs. When resources are tight, school administrators revise school budgets, excluding curriculum extras such as peer mediation and peace studies programs. Results from the Comprehensive Peer Mediation Project (CPMEP) overwhelmingly indicate that peer mediation programs "provide significant benefit in developing constructive social and conflict behavior in children at all educational levels" (Jones, 1998, p. 18). Ironically, we are cutting the very school programs that have the potential to improve learning climates that ultimately could raise national test scores.

Peer mediation programs train students as neutral third parties to intervene and assist other students in the resolution and management of interpersonal disputes (Jones and Brinkman, 1994). Typically, the training is approximately fifteen hours of learning about interpersonal conflict, active listening, paraphrasing, reframing, and role playing (Jones and Brinkman, 1994; Burrell and Vogl, 1990). Student mediators encourage their peers to explore issues systematically and to do problem solving collaboratively. The goal of peer interventions is to generate agreements acceptable to everyone and to develop a strategy to handle similar problems in the future.

This meta-analysis of mediation outcomes in schools reviews existing studies of mediation practices in elementary and secondary schools employing a problem-solving approach to mediation. The meta-analysis examines the effectiveness of mediation (ability to reach agreements and satisfaction of the participants) and related outcomes in educational settings (positive impact on school climate, perceptions of the level of conflict in the school, reduction in behavior requiring disciplinary action).

Issues in School-Based Mediation Programs

To review studies evaluating mediation programs in school settings, several components were identified and measured. The broad categories for outcome measures included behavioral indicators of conflict for students, mediation outcomes that reflected how many conflicts were resolved and agreements reached, student and teacher perceptions about conflict and individual attitudes toward conflict in the school, and personality factors related to conflict resolution such as student self-concept or self-esteem. In addition, since the school mediation programs followed a problem-solving approach, much emphasis was placed on the training and use of communication skills, understanding the dynamics of conflict, and identifying specific conflict strategies that could be used when dealing with conflict.

Specific research studies looked at various aspects of these broader components. For behavioral indicators, the types of conflict among students, the nature or intensity of the disputes, or the frequency of conflict situations occurring on school property were identified (Johnson, Johnson, Mitchell, Cotton, Harris, and Louison, 1996; Roush and Hall, 1993; Lindsay, 1998; Johnson, Johnson, Dudley, and Acikgoz, 1994; Johnson, Johnson, and Dudley, 1992; Johnson, Johnson, Cotton, Harris, and Louison, 1995; Johnson, Johnson, Dudley, Ward, and Magnuson, 1995; Hart and Gunty, 1997; Bodtker and Jones, 1997). The types and frequencies of conflict reported may include such acts as physical aggression, insults, playground issues, or problems with turn taking (Johnson, Johnson, Dudley, Ward, and Magnuson, 1995). One study looked at mediation skill transference from the school to the home environment and identified behavioral indicators of conflict within the home and how the student mediators addressed them (Gentry and Benenson, 1993). The suggestion that students who are trained in conflict resolution strategies apply those skills to settings that are external to the school environment in which they were learned (Johnson, Johnson, and Dudley, 1992) implies that training students can have longer-lasting impact and affect wider audiences (siblings, families, and the community at large). Unfortunately, the lack of data on this point does not permit inclusion of this feature as part of the meta-analysis. The potential transference of skills points to a target area for future research studies on the impact of mediation in the schools.

Many school-based mediation programs follow a process in which peer mediators (third-party neutrals) work with disputing students to help them through a process in order to achieve resolution, something that is easily measured by the number of agreements reached for the number of mediations attempted (Araki, 1990; Crary, 1992; Daunic and others, 2000; Hart and Gunty, 1997; Johnson, Johnson, Mitchell, Cotton, Harris, and Louison, 1996; Johnson, Johnson, Cotton, Harris, and Louison, 1995; Roush and Hall, 1993). Similarly, the satisfaction of participants involved in the mediation process is easily measured and generally results in highly positive satisfaction findings (Crary, 1992; Gerber, 1999; Hart and Gunty, 1997; Johnson, Thomas, and Krochak, 1998).

Since the basic premise of many school-based mediation programs is that conflict resolution strategies can be taught to students, and knowledge about these resolution strategies can then be applied to conflict situations and results effected, it is important to determine the degree to which this training is effective and the ages at which training can occur. Studies differentiate between learning about various conflict strategies and how they might be used in conflict situations (Bodtker and Jones, 1997; Johnson, Johnson, Dudley, Mitchell, and Fredreickson, 1997; Johnson, Johnson, Dudley, and Magnuson, 1996; Stevahn, Johnson, Johnson, Laginski, and O'Coin, 1996) and the actual ability to apply appropriate conflict resolution knowledge and strategies in specific situations (Gentry and Benenson, 1993; Johnson, Johnson, and Dudley, 1992; Stevahn, Johnson, Johnson, Green, and Laginski, 1997), or the presence of both attributes (Johnson, Johnson, Dudley, and Acikgoz, 1994; Johnson, Johnson, Dudley, and Magnuson, 1995; Johnson, Johnson, Dudley, Ward, and Magnuson, 1995; Stevahn, Johnson, Johnson, and Real, 1996).

The idea that conflict resolution strategies and participation in school-based mediation programs potentially affect self-concept and self-esteem in students presents an intriguing concept for expectations of a problem-solving approach to mediation. Several studies looked at the effects of mediation programs on student self-esteem or teacher perception of changed self-concept, mostly with inconclusive results (Crary, 1992; Gentry and Benenson, 1993; Roush and Hall, 1993; Vanayan, White, Yuen, and Teper, 1996). Combining the results from these individual studies and testing them through the meta-analytic process produces a clearer understanding of statistical significance. However, some of the studies question the selection of student mediators and the potential to recognize the greatest gains in changed self-concept among students who initially had lower self-esteem (Roush and Hall, 1993; Vanayan, White, Yuen, and Teper, 1996).

Related to student changes in self-esteem are measurements on conflict orientation and changes in school climate as a result of mediation program interventions. Orientation to conflict refers to student perceptions about the nature of conflict and resulting outcomes. Is conflict viewed as a problem, or an opportunity for change? Does the perception of conflict resolution connote a win-lose or a win-win outcome? Since conflict represents an inevitable component of student life, being able to positively affect perceptions of conflict and the importance of constructive resolution strategies presents a key to long-term changes in student behavior and the overall impact on school climate. Though some studies cite anecdotal evidence supporting positive changes in conflict orientation and school climate (Johnson, Johnson, Dudley, and Magnuson, 1995; Johnson, Johnson, Dudley, and Magnuson, 1996), only a few report statistical data related to school climate (Lindsay, 1998; Bodtker and Jones, 1997; Hart and Gunty, 1997).

A final area that has been included in the school-based mediation research involves conflict knowledge and influencing positive perceptions of conflict (Stevahn, Johnson, Johnson, Laginski, and O'Coin, 1996; Stevahn, Johnson, Johnson, and Real, 1996). Some of the studies specifically measured the improved knowledge about conflict through the effective conflict resolution strategies employed in handling them (Johnson, Johnson, Dudley, Mitchell, and Fredreickson, 1997; Johnson, Johnson, Dudley, and Acikgoz, 1994; Johnson, Johnson, and Dudley, 1992; Stevahn, Johnson, Johnson, Green, and Laginski, 1997). When students better understand the dynamics of conflict, they are better equipped to deal constructively with conflict resolution and use appropriate skills in handling conflict.

Although there are many supporters of school-based mediation programs, critics have surfaced (Gerber, 1999; Webster, 1993). Research supporting school mediation programs has been criticized as being "primarily anecdotal and supplied by teachers and administrators, who report that peer mediation programs reduce suspension and detention rates" (Johnson, Johnson, Dudley, Ward, and Magnuson, 1995, p. 832). Other critics claim there is no evidence that mediation programs reduce interpersonal violence, but rather that the programs provide political cover for politicians and school officials, distracting the public from the structural determinants of youth violence (Webster, 1993).

Methods

This section describes the selection of literature and the meta-analytic techniques.

Literature Research Description

To be included in the meta-analysis, studies needed to possess these characteristics:

- Include students in an educational facility encompassing one or more grade levels between kindergarten and high school senior year as the sample population in the research.
- Use quantitative research methodologies resulting in numerical representation of measurable effects or outcomes.
- Involve at least one variable relating to mediation training or practices among student peers in which outcomes or effects of the training or actual mediation procedures were measured.

Data from forty-three studies meeting the inclusion criteria (indicated by asterisks in the references) were included in this meta-analysis from the examination of more than two hundred manuscripts generated by the search. Data sets appearing in multiple manuscripts were entered only once in the database. Data sets ranged in date from 1985 to the present. Manuscripts were eliminated from the study if they did not meet these criteria or if they relied on research with no quantitative data (the case with Chetkow-Yanoov, 1996; Harris, 1996; Heller, 1996; Hill, 1996; Nor, 1996), evaluated comparative data among training practices without measuring

Table 1. Summary of Studies Used in the Analysis

Study (Lead) Author	Date	Grade[1]	No. of Mediations	No. (Percentage) of Agreement	Effect Size	Outcome Type[2]
Araki	1990	H, I, E	136	133 (98)	.000	SC
Bodtker and Jones	1997	H			.000	CSU
Bradley	1989	H	65	62 (95)	-.333	SR
Casella	2000	H				
Crary	1992	I	95	92 (97)	-.043	TPC
					.010	SE
Daunic, Smith, Robinson, Landry, and Miller	2000	I	165	157 (95)		
Davis, A.	1986	H	290	236 (81)	-.222	SR
Davis, G.	1994	H			-.333	SR
Gentry and Benenson	1993	I			.397	CSU
					-.417	SR
					.235	SE
Hart and Gunty	1997	E	350	340 (97)	-.042	SR
Johnson, Johnson, Mitchell, Cotton, Harris, and Louison	1996	E	323	317 (98)		
Johnson, Johnson, Cotton, Harris, and Louison	1995	E	290	309 (94)		
Johnson, Johnson, and Dudley	1992	E			.670	FM
					.330	TPC

Johnson, Johnson, Dudley, and Acikgoz	1994	E			.889	FM
					.831	CSU
					−.200	TPC
					−.200	SR
Johnson, Johnson, Dudley, and Magnuson	1995	E			.546	FM
					.415	CSU
Johnson, Johnson, Dudley, and Magnuson	1996	E			.552	MKC
					.436	CSU
Johnson, Johnson, Dudley, Mitchell, and Fredreickson	1997	I			.811	MKC
					.426	CSU
Johnson, Johnson, Dudley, Ward, and Magnuson	1995	E			.275	FM
					.268	CSU
Jones and Brinkman	1998	E, I, H	358	315 (88)	−.120	SR
Kinasewitz	1996	H	24	21 (88)	−.250	SR
Kirleis	1995	H			.426	CSU
Kolan	1999	H	120	111 (93)	.372	MVC
Lam	1989	–	13	13 (100)	−.215	SR
Payne	1993	–	271	241 (89)	.544	MKC
Rousch and Hall	1993	E, I	52	50 (96)	−.400	SR
Sherrod	1995				−.333	SR
Smart	1987	H, I			−.330	SR
Stader and Johnson	1999	H	67	52 (78)	.365	SC
Stern	1986	I			.472	SE
Stevahn, Johnson, Johnson, Green, and Laginski	1997	H			.429	AA
					.589	MKC

(Continued)

Table 1. Summary of Studies Used in the Analysis (Continued)

Study (Lead) Author	Date	Grade[1]	No. of Mediations	No. (Percentage) of Agreement	Effect Size	Outcome Type[2]
					.793	FM
					.433	CSU
					.329	MVC
Stevahn, Johnson, Johnson, Laginski, and O'Coin	1996	H			.360	AA
					.793	MKC
					.802	CSU
					.259	MVC
Stevahn, Johnson, Johnson, and Real	1996	E, I			.410	AA
					.960	MKC
					.347	CSU
Terry and Gerber	1997	H	39	39 (100)		
Tolson and McDonald	1992	H			−.366	SR
Vanayan, White, Yuen, and Teper	1996	I			.118	SE
					.118	SC
					.118	MKC
					.118	SR
Webne-Behrman	1989	H, I	56	42 (75)		

Note: Several studies provided estimates from multiple samples; the estimate reported in this table is the average estimate for the combined study. Individual estimates may be obtained from the authors.

[1]The letter indicates the level of grades in the analysis, where E = elementary, I = intermediate, and H = high school.
[2]The type of dependent variable provided is as follows: SC indicates school climate, TPC = teacher perception of conflict, SR = use of school disciplinary records, MKC = mediator's level of knowledge about conflict, FM = ability to follow directions about how to mediate, CSU = type of conflict strategy used, MVC = mediator view of conflict, AA = academic record, and SE = level of self-esteem.

training outcomes, included measures for mediation predictors such as hostile environment or bullying without evaluating mediated interventions (Whitney and Smith, 1993), reported no sample size (Thompson, 1996), or relied on sample populations drawn from university students or communities at large (Johnson, 1967; Leadbeater, Hellner, Allen, and Aber, 1989; Ross, Fischer, Baker, and Buchholz, 1997).

Coding of Program Outcomes

The outcomes implementing mediation programs and training were divided into four general categories: (1) descriptive outcomes, (2) impact on the schools, (3) issues related to conflict resolution, and (4) impact on the mediator.

Descriptive outcomes consisted of two aspects of mediation: percentage of successful mediations or agreements reached, and satisfaction with the overall agreement. When assessing mediation programs, tracking the number of agreements that occurred is important for continued support of school administrators, teachers, and staff. If agreement was reached, then the students' problems have been addressed. In addition, in order for any program to maintain support, it is paramount that participants be satisfied with the outcomes and overall process.

The second category centered on the overall impact of mediation training or program on the schools. There were three measures in this cluster: students' perceptions of school climate related to conflict; teachers' and administrators' perceptions of the school conflict climate; and behavioral indicators such as fighting, suspensions, expulsions, and other disciplinary actions. This combination of measures indicates the level of conflict, both perceptual and behavioral, from students' and adults' perspectives.

The third category relates to the impact of mediation training on mediators' views about interpersonal conflict. Four measures were included in this cluster: knowledge about conflict, ability to follow procedures during a mediation session, strategies used to resolve conflict, and view of interpersonal conflict. The first measure reflects whether the training increased participants' knowledge about conflict. The second measure indexed trainees' ability to facilitate a mediation session using guidelines established by the program. The third measure indicates the general strategies mediators use to address conflict. The fourth measure in this cluster evaluates whether student mediators view interpersonal conflict positively or negatively.

The last category focuses on the impact of mediation training on trainees. Two measures in this category are academic achievement and self-esteem. The purpose of these measures is to determine the impact of mediation training on participants. Program evaluators wanted to know if students' grades might improve with mediation training and whether participants might feel better about themselves.

Statistical Procedure

Three stages occurred in this analysis: (1) transformation, (2) averaging, and (3) heterogeneity testing. This meta-analytic review used the variance-centered technique developed by Hunter and Schmidt (1990). Transformation is the process of converting statistical information to a common metric. The correlation coefficient is the metric used in this review. In short, all of the studies' statistical information was transformed into correlation coefficients as outlined by Hunter and Schmidt. The second stage was the averaging process, which computes a weighted average using the sample size of the individual effect as the weight. Finally, testing for homogeneity was the third step in this process. The homogeneity test examines whether the inconsistency in observed effects can be attributed to sampling error. A chi-square test compares the observed variability to the expected variability to sampling error. A nonsignificant chi square indicates that the sample of correlations can be considered homogeneous, whereas a significant chi square indicates heterogeneity among the effects.

Results

Results of the meta-analysis reveal important contributions of peer mediation programs.

Descriptive Outcomes of Mediation Programs

The first step is to analyze the ability of the program to resolve disagreements. The obvious goal of mediation programs is to give students an opportunity to resolve conflicts with their peers rather than to have an adult solve their problems for them. Twenty-three studies report the results of 4,327 mediations, with 4,028 reaching agreement (for a 93 percent success rate). This high percentage of agreements reached indicates the success of mediation programs in the schools.

However, reaching an agreement is not the only index of a successful program. Disputants must also feel satisfied with the process itself. Fifteen studies report survey data on 4,739 mediations. The results indicate that

4,191 of the disputants in mediation are satisfied with the agreement, for an 88 percent satisfaction rate. Again, this high percentage indicates not only that agreements have been reached but also that participants were pleased with the outcomes of their mediation process. It may also be the case that students feel empowered to resolve their own disputes rather than being told how to solve their problems by an adult.

Impact of Mediation Programs on Schools

The first outcome measure from the perception of students is how they view their school climate. Five studies examine the impact of mediation programs on school climate and find that mediation programs have a positive effect on school climates ($r = .441$, $k = 5$, $N = 527$, $p < .05$). These results indicate that students perceive a positive school environment. The test of homogeneity finds the sample of correlations heterogeneous, $\chi^2 = 20.61$ $(4, N = 527)$, $p < .05$. Because of heterogeneity, the average correlation should be interpreted cautiously. An examination was made for outlier studies. One estimate (Bodtker and Jones, 1997) had a correlation entry of .000. This estimate was based on their reporting of a nonsignificant finding and was the best reasonable estimate of the relationship. When compared to the average estimate, it has a z score in excess of 4.00, indicating that the study functions as an outlier. Reestimating the average effect ($r = .441$, $k = 4$, $N = 443$, $p > .05$) creates a homogeneous set of correlations $\chi^2 = 4.86$ $(3, N = 443)$, $p > .05$. In short, these findings indicate that school climates improve after the implementation of a mediation program. A complete summary of all the findings involving average r calculations is found in Table 2.

A second measure centers on teachers' and administrators' perception of conflict in their respective schools. The results indicate that a mediation program reduces the perception of conflict in a school ($r = -.093$, $k = 4$, $N = 379$, $p < .05$). In other words, both teachers and administrators perceive a reduction in conflict. The test of homogeneity finds the sample of correlations homogeneous, $\chi^2 = 2.15$ $(3, N = 379)$, $p > .05$. The studies consistently find that both teachers and administrators perceive a reduction in conflict. These results indicate that professionals, on a day-to-day basis, attribute less conflict after implementing mediation programs.

A third systemic measure deals with data from school records such as suspensions, expulsions, fighting, and other disciplinary actions. The implication of mediation programs is a drop in disciplinary actions

Table 2. Summary Data Information

	Average Correlation	Standard Error	95% CI for r	z Statistic Test for r	Homogeneity Test of Sample
Impact on school					
School climate	.441	.198	±.388	2.23*	20.61*
Conflict perception	−.093	.075	±.147	1.24	2.15
School records	−.287	.117	±.221	2.49*	77.22*
Conflict change					
Knowledge	.530	.218	±.427	2.43*	53.84*
Follow directions	.495	.208	±.407	2.38*	37.74*
Strategies used	.410	.215	±.422	1.91	61.11*
View of conflict	.341	.106	±.207	3.22*	3.81
Impact on mediator					
Academic	.404	.028	±.056	14.43*	0.18
Self-esteem	.110	.133	±.261	.83	4.19

Note: * = results that are statistically significant at the $p < .05$ level.

required by administrators ($r = -.287$, $k = 17$, $N = 5,706$, $p < .05$). These results indicate that the implementation of a mediation program is related to a drop in administrative suspensions, expulsions, and disciplinary actions. The test of homogeneity finds the sample of correlations heterogeneous, $\chi^2 = 77.22$ (16, $N = 5,706$), $p < .05$. Because of heterogeneity, the average correlation should be interpreted cautiously. Heterogeneity means that the sample of correlations does not represent a single distribution but instead indicates the probability of moderator variables. However, sixteen of the seventeen effects were positive, suggesting that any moderator variable would be indicating differences between small positive and large positive effects. Therefore, the average effect even after considering a moderator variable will always be positive. In short, the data indicate a reduction in disciplinary actions after the implementation of mediation programs.

Issues Related to Conflict

The next set of measures reflect peer mediators' perceptions about conflict. The first measure, knowledge about conflict, reflects what students learned about interpersonal conflict from their mediation training ($r = .530$, $k = 14$, $N = 1,138$, $p < .05$). These results indicate that students' knowledge and understanding about interpersonal conflict increased from their training. The test of homogeneity finds the sample of correlations heterogeneous, $\chi^2 = 53.84$ (13, $N = 1,138$), $p < .05$. The range in correlations is $r = .118$ to $r = .960$, which indicates a large variability. The variability in knowledge gained about conflict may reflect differences in mediation training programs, content of the knowledge tests, and different selection processes of mediators between school districts.

A second measure centered on students' ability to follow the steps prescribed in mediating a dispute. Results ($r = .495$, $k = 9$, $N = 805$, $p < .05$) indicate that students are indeed able to follow the steps in mediating interpersonal conflicts. The test of homogeneity finds the sample of correlations heterogeneous, $\chi^2 = 34.74$ (8, $N = 805$), $p < .05$. Because of heterogeneity, the average correlation should be interpreted cautiously. These findings may index differences in the simplicity or complexity of the mediation training programs.

A third measure centered on the strategies mediators used to resolve interpersonal conflict. Results show that mediation training changes the way mediators address interpersonal conflicts and disputes ($r = .410$, $k = 15$, $N = 1,318$, $p < .05$). The test of homogeneity finds the sample of correlations heterogeneous, $\chi^2 = 61.11$ (15, $N = 1,318$), $p < .05$. These findings, although heterogeneous, reflect a distribution of all positive effects. Therefore the average effect demonstrates that mediators' intervention strategies were consistent with the training.

A fourth measure centered on mediators' view of conflict (either positive or negative). Results of mediation training indicate an increased positive view of conflict from peer mediators' perspectives ($r = .341$, $k = 5$, $N = 297$, $p < .05$). The test of homogeneity finds the sample of correlations homogeneous, $\chi^2 = 3.81$ (4, $N = 341$), $p > .05$. These findings indicate that student mediators' perceptions of conflict were more positive after their training.

Impact of Training and Being a Mediator

These two measures look at the impact of both training and being a peer mediator for a year. The first measure centers on academic achievement of mediators. Results show that peer mediators' grades went up ($r = .404$, $k = 4$, $N = 223$, $p < .05$). The test of homogeneity finds the sample of correlations homogeneous, $\chi^2 = 0.18$ (3, $N = 223$), $p < .05$. These findings indicate a substantial increase in academic performance after becoming a mediator.

A second measure centered on mediators' self-esteem. Results indicate that peer mediators' sense of self improved over the academic year ($r = .110$, $k = 4$, $N = 237$, $p < .05$). In other words, by being a school mediator the student's sense of self improved. The test of homogeneity finds the sample of correlations homogeneous, $\chi^2 = 4.19$ (3, $N = 237$), $p > .05$. Similarly, these findings point to improved self-esteem after becoming a mediator.

Discussion

The results of this meta-analytic review of school-based mediation programs overwhelmingly support the effectiveness of mediation programs in educational settings. The study demonstrates that student training on understanding conflict situations and learning appropriate conflict resolution strategies to help students resolve conflict can be successfully implemented in elementary and secondary schools. Basically, conflict resolution skills can be taught to students, and students can effectively demonstrate the use of these skills in mediating peer conflicts and helping disputants reach agreement. Student satisfaction with the peer mediation process is highly positive for mediation programs. Ideally, this conclusion will encourage schools without mediation programs to implement a peer mediation program to manage interpersonal conflict.

The question of how important the findings of the studies are for practical application can best be expressed using the Binomial Effect Size Display (BESD), developed by Rosenthal for expressing average effects generated by meta-analysis (Rosenthal, 1984). A complete BESD display of the findings appears in Table 3. This representation demonstrates the importance and impact of the change that the presence of a mediation program should be expected to produce in a school. The smallest change is a 22 percent increase for self-esteem and a 22 percent decrease in the teachers' perceptions of conflict at school. Interestingly, the actual school records indicate a larger diminished level of behavioral problems (68 percent) than the perceptual measures. The representation in the table should leave little doubt about the importance of the size of the average effects estimated. The next step, as suggested by Sandy (2001), should be a concentration on establishing "best practices" to facilitate the implementation of programs. The results indicate only that the presence of the program produces a desirable outcome, without providing information on what constitutes optimal

Table 3. Binomial Effect Size Display for Interpreting Results

		Percentage Above (Below) Median		
	Size Effect	No Program	Mediation Program	Percentage Increase (Decrease)
School climate	.441	28	72	157
Perception conflict level	−.093	45.5	55.5	22
School records	−.285	36	64	68
Mediator knowledge	.530	23.5	76.5	225
Ability to follow steps	.495	25	75	200
Conflict resolution strategies	.410	30	70	133
View of conflict	.341	33	67	103
Academic achievement	.404	30	70	133
Self-esteem	.110	45	55	22

practice. Future research should address how the outcomes produced by the introduction of a program can best be realized.

On the basis of this study, it can be said that an important direction for future researchers would be to look at the degree to which student mediators used their intervention training outside of school settings. That is, do students use the problem-solving skills (active listening, question asking, reframing) in family and neighborhood interactions? The transference of conflict resolution skills extends into families and communities, presenting unique opportunities for young adults to potentially affect social change in family structures and in neighborhoods. Very few studies looked specifically at student skills in handling sibling conflict within family structures, but perhaps further monitoring of students could reflect long-term behavioral changes that pervade social networks of peers and neighbors. Learning how to manage conflict is a powerful resource for young adults to handle many of life's challenges, and the successful use of conflict resolution strategies continuously reinforces the value and benefit of constructive problem solving. Beyond providing relief for students, these skills can powerfully demonstrate to others involved in their interactions the positive effects of communication and negotiation efforts.

Another intriguing area for future research involves a question proposed by several researchers in trying to measure changes in student self-esteem and school climate as a result of mediation programs. American schools today, in general, enjoy an all-time low level of school violence. Is there a connection between the introduction of school-based mediation programs and a reduction in school violence? Is there a significant difference between schools with and without mediation programs that cannot be attributed to other socioeconomic or demographic factors?

Looking at self-esteem, several studies noted anecdotal data about increased self-esteem among student participants trained in mediation programs, particularly among those mediators who themselves had behavioral problems and frequent episodes of conflict at school. Since no hard data exist to determine conclusively whether at-risk students benefit more than non-at-risk students from training on conflict resolution skills, studies that determine the effectiveness of targeted training interventions can help schools achieve even greater gains in improving school climates and mediation satisfaction, particularly by enriching the lives of at-risk students.

Finally, our challenge in the next decade is to conduct useful research validating school-based mediation and curriculum-based conflict resolution programs. Data from the Comprehensive Peer Mediation Evaluation Project (CPMEP) indicates that using peer mediation reduces conflict and aggressiveness and increases prosocial values, conflict competence, and perspective taking (Jones, 1998). Educators are charged with helping students develop their academic skills, but facilitating students' emotional intelligence is equally essential to their success in the world. Clearly, our goal as scholars and researchers is to persuade school policy makers and decision makers that conflict resolution education is in everyone's best interest through well-framed empirical research and curriculum development.

References

References marked with an asterisk indicate studies included in the meta-analysis.

*Araki, C. T. "Dispute Management in the Schools." *Mediation Quarterly,* 1990, *8* (1), 51–62.

*Bodtker, A. M., and Jones, T. S. "The Impact of Peer Mediation Training on Conflict Competence: Insights from South African Students." Paper presented at the 83rd Annual Meeting of the National Communication Association, Chicago, Nov. 1997.

*Bradley, B. "Warwick Valley Students Learn to Mediate." *Journal of the New York State School Boards Association,* 1989, *4,* 17–18.

Burrell, N. A., and Vogl, S. M. "Turf-Side Conflict Mediation for Students." *Mediation Quarterly,* 1990, *7* (3), 237–252.

*Casella, R. "The Benefits of Peer Mediation in the Context of Urban Conflict and Program Status." *Urban Education,* 2000, *35* (3), 324–356.

Chetkow-Yanoov, B. "Conflict Resolution Skills Can Be Taught." *Peabody Journal of Education,* 1996, *71* (3), 12–28.

*Crary, D. R. "Community Benefits from Mediation: A Test of the 'Peace Virus' Hypothesis." *Mediation Quarterly,* 1992, *9* (3), 241–252.

*Daunic, A. P., Smith, S. W., Robinson, T. R., Landry, K. L., and Miller, M. D. "School-Wide Conflict Resolution and Peer Mediation Programs: Experiences in Three Middle Schools." *Intervention in School and Clinic,* 2000, *36* (2), 94–101.

*Davis, A. M. "Teaching Ideas: Dispute Resolution at an Early Age." *Negotiation Journal,* 1986, *2,* 287–298.

*Davis, G. M. "Don't Fight: Mediate." *Journal of Invitational Theory and Practice,* 1994, *3,* 85–94.

*Eisler, J. *Comprehensive Conflict Resolution Training Program, 1993–1994.* New York: Office of Educational Research Report, New York City Board of Education, 1994. (ERIC document no. 380 749)

*Gentry, D. B., and Benenson, W. A. "School-Age Peer Mediators Transfer Knowledge and Skills to Home Setting." *Mediation Quarterly,* 1993, *10* (1), 101–109.

*Gerber, S. "Does Peer Mediation Really Work?" *Professional School Counseling,* 1999, *2* (3), 169–172.

Harris, I. "Peace Education in an Urban School District in the United States." *Peabody Journal of Education,* 1996, *71* (3), 63–83.

*Hart, J., and Gunty, M. "The Impact of a Peer Mediation Program on an Elementary School Environment." *Peace and Change,* 1997, *22* (1), 76–92.

*Heller, G. S. "Changing the School to Reduce Student Violence: What Works?" *NASSP Bulletin,* 1996, *80* (579), 1–10.

Hill, M. S. "Making Students Part of the Safe Schools Solution." *NASSP Bulletin,* 1996, *80* (579), 24–31.

Hunter, J. E., and Schmidt, F. L. *Methods of Meta-Analysis: Correcting Error and Bias in Research Findings.* Thousand Oaks, Calif.: Sage, 1990.

Johnson, D. W. "Use of Role Reversal in Intergroup Competition." *Journal of Personality and Social Psychology,* 1967, *7* (2), 135–141.

*Johnson, D. W., and Johnson, R. T. "Teaching All Students How to Manage Conflicts Constructively: The Peacemaker's Program." *Journal of Negro Education,* 1996, *65,* 322–334.

*Johnson, D. W., and Johnson, R. T. "Conflict Resolution and Peer Mediation Programs in Elementary and Secondary Schools: A Review of the Research." *Review of Educational Research,* 1996, *66* (4), 459–506.

*Johnson, D. W., Johnson, R. T., Cotton, B., Harris, D., and Louison, S. "Using Conflict Managers in an Inner-City Elementary School." *Mediation Quarterly,* 1995, *12* (4), 379–390.

*Johnson, D. W., Johnson, R. T., and Dudley, B., "Effects of Peer Mediation Training on Elementary School Students." *Mediation Quarterly,* 1992, *10,* 89–99.

*Johnson, D. W., Johnson, R. T., Dudley, B., and Acikgoz, K. "Effects of Conflict Resolution Training on Elementary School Students." *Journal of Social Psychology,* 1994, *134,* 803–817.

*Johnson, D. W., Johnson, R. T., Dudley, B., and Magnuson, D. "Training Elementary Schools to Manage Conflict." *Journal of Social Psychology,* 1995, *135* (6), 673–680.

*Johnson, D. W., Johnson, R. T., Dudley, B., and Magnuson, D. "Training Elementary Schools to Manage Conflict." *Journal of Group Psychotherapy, Psychodrama and Sociometry,* 1996, *49* (1), 24–39.

*Johnson, D. W., Johnson, R. T., Dudley, B., Mitchell, J., and Fredreickson, J. "The Impact of Conflict Resolution Training on Middle School Students." *Journal of Social Psychology,* 1997, *137* (1), 11–22.

*Johnson, D. W., Johnson, R. T., Dudley, B., Ward, M., and Magnuson, D. "The Impact of Peer Mediation Training on the Management of School and Home Conflicts." *American Educational Research Journal,* 1995, *32* (4), 829–844.

*Johnson, D. W., Johnson, R. T., Mitchell, J., Cotton, B., Harris, D., and Louison, S. "Effectiveness of Conflict Managers in an Inner-City Elementary School." *Journal of Educational Research,* 1996, *89* (5), 280–285.

*Johnson, E. A., Thomas, D., and Krochak, D. "Effects of Peer Mediation Training in Junior High School on Mediators' Conflict Resolution Attitudes and Abilities in High School." *Alberta Journal of Educational Research,* 1998, *44* (3), 339–341.

*Jones, T. "Research Supports Effectiveness of Peer Mediation." *The Fourth R: The Newsletter of the National Association for Mediation in Education,* 1998, *4* (Mar.–Apr.), 1ff.

Jones, T. S., and Brinkman, H. "Teach Your Children Well: Recommendations for Peer Mediation Programs." In J. P. Folger and T. S. Jones (eds.), *New Directions in Mediation.* Thousand Oaks, Calif.: Sage, 1994.

*Kinasewitz, T. *Reducing Aggression in a High School Setting Through a Conflict Resolution and Peer Mediation Program.* Ed.D. practicum for Nova Southeastern University, 1996. (ERIC document no. 400 495)

*Kirleis, K. *The Effects of Peer Mediation Training on Conflicts Among Behaviorally and Emotionally Disordered High School Students.* Practicum report submitted to the Abraham S. Fischler Center for the Advancement of Education of Nova Southeastern degree of Educational Specialist, 1995. (ERIC document no. 394 865)

*Kolan, K. "An Analysis of the Short-Term Impact of Peer Mediation on High School Disputants in an Ethnically Diverse Suburban School System." Unpublished doctoral dissertation, George Washington University, Washington, D.C., 1999. (ERIC document no. 430 168)

*Lam, J. A. *The Impact of Conflict Resolution Programs on Schools: A Review and Synthesis of the Evidence* (2nd ed.). Amherst: University of Massachusetts, 1989.

Leadbeater, B. J., Hellner, I., Allen, J. P., and Aber, J. L. "Assessment of Interpersonal Negotiation Strategies in Youth Engaged in Problem Behaviors." *Developmental Psychology*, 1989, *25* (3), 465–472.

*Lindsay, P. "Conflict Resolution and Peer Mediation in Public Schools: What Works?" *Mediation Quarterly*, 1998, *16* (1), 85–99.

*Maxwell, J. "Mediation in the Schools: Self-Regulation, Self-Esteem, and Self-Discipline." *Mediation Quarterly*, 1989, *7* (2), 149–155.

*Nor, L. "Taking a Stand Against Violence. Leadership and Responsibility: One School's Quest to Create a Safe Harbor." *Schools in the Middle*, 1996, *5* (4), 14–17.

Rosenthal, R. *Meta-Analytic Procedures for Social Research.* Thousand Oaks, Calif.: Sage, 1984.

*Ross, W. H., Jr., Fischer, D., Baker, C., and Buchholz, K. "University Residence Hall Assistants as Mediators: An Investigation of the Effects of Disputant and Mediator Relationships on Intervention Preferences." *Journal of Applied Social Psychology*, 1997, *27* (8), 664–707.

*Roush, G., and Hall, E. "Teaching Peaceful Conflict Resolution." *Mediation Quarterly*, 1993, *11* (2), 185–191.

*Sandy, S. "Conflict Resolution Education in the Schools: 'Getting There.'" *Conflict Resolution Quarterly*, 2001, *19* (2), 237–250.

*Stader, D., and Johnson, J. "Reducing Violence in High School." Paper presented at the Second Joint National/School Community Conference on Youth Violence and Substance Abuse, Kissimmee, Fla., Nov. 1999. (ERIC document no. 444 085)

Stevahn, L., Johnson, D. W., Johnson, R., Green, K., and Laginski, A. "Effects of Conflict Resolution Training Integrated into English Literature on High School Students." *Journal of Social Psychology*, 1997, *137* (3), 302–315.

*Stevahn, L., Johnson, D. W., Johnson, R., Laginski, A. M., and O'Coin, I. "Effects on High School Students of Integrating Conflict Resolution and Peer Mediation Training into an Academic Unit." *Mediation Quarterly*, 1996, *14* (1), 21–36.

*Stevahn, L., Johnson, D. W., Johnson, R., and Real, D. "The Impact of a Cooperative or Individualistic Context on the Effectiveness of Conflict Resolution Training." *American Educational Research Journal*, 1996, *33* (3), 801–823.

Thompson, S. "Peer Mediation: A Peaceful Solution." *School Counselor*, 1996, *44* (2), 151–155.

*Vanayan, M., White, N., Yuen, P., and Teper, M. "The Effects of a School-Based Mediation Program on the Attitudes and Perceptions of Student Mediators." *Education Canada*, 1996, 38–42.

Vanayan, M., White, N., Yuen, P., and Teper, M. "Would You Like to Be a Peer Mediator? Willingness to Be a Peer Mediator Among Elementary Students: Effects of Grade and Gender." *Alberta Journal of Educational Research*, 1997, *43* (1), 57–60.

Volpe, M. R., and Witherspoon, R. "Mediation and Cultural Diversity on College Campuses." *Mediation Quarterly,* 1992, *9* (4), 341–351.

Webster, D. "The Unconvincing Case for School-Based Conflict Resolution Programs for Adolescents." *Health Affairs,* 1993, *1,* 127–141.

Whitney, L., and Smith, P. "A Survey of the Nature and Extent of Bully/Victim Problems in Junior/Middle and Secondary Schools." *Educational Research,* 1993, *35,* 3–25.

Nancy A. Burrell is an associate professor in the Communication Department at the University of Wisconsin-Milwaukee. Her research centers on managing interpersonal conflict in educational, organizational, and family contexts. She has edited three books and published in *Human Communication Research, American Journal of Distance Communication and Family,* and *Conciliation Courts Review.* She is director of the Mediation Center at UW-Milwaukee.

Cindy S. Zirbel completed her M.A. in 2001, earned a graduate certificate in mediation and negotiation, and was project assistant for the Mediation Center at the University of Wisconsin-Milwaukee. Recently, she completed a book chapter on issues in peer mediation and is working as a financial consultant.

Mike Allen is a professor at the University of Wisconsin-Milwaukee. His research centers on social influence in organizational, interpersonal, and mass media contexts. He has published more than one hundred works, including three books and articles appearing in *Psychological Bulletin, Communication Monographs, Law and Human Behavior,* and *Education and the Health Professions.* He is the current editor of *Communication Studies.*

Conflict Resolution and Moral Reasoning

WARREN R. HEYDENBERK
ROBERTA ANNA HEYDENBERK
SHARON PERKINS BAILEY

The effects of conflict resolution training on students' moral reasoning were examined in this five-year study. Inspired by pilot studies that found increased attachment, cooperation, and prosocial skills in treatment classrooms, the study was conducted with elementary students (ten treatment groups and eight comparison groups) in a low-income Philadelphia school and in two schools in a suburban low-income district. Treatment group teachers were trained in integrated conflict resolution strategies, and they were provided ongoing support to ensure classroom implementation of conflict resolution skills. Treatment group students demonstrated significant improvement in moral reasoning.

School violence and antisocial behavior in American schools have inspired numerous conflict resolution curricula over the last two decades. By 1998, the majority of American schools had mandated conflict resolution programs (Nemecek, 1998). Although a host of research affirms the value of conflict resolution and peer mediation programs in promoting prosocial student behavior, some critical areas have gone unquestioned.

Indices of moral reasoning are reflected in conflict resolution researchers' dependent variables, among them verbal aggression, physical altercations, and behavioral referrals by teachers. Improvement in student behavior that subsumes moral reasoning has been posited by conflict resolution researchers (Crawford and Bodine, 1996). Although the indices are not labeled as moral reasoning, these criteria operationally represent what is defined by the researchers to be moral reasoning.

The comprehensive conflict resolution classroom is an opportunity for students to reason and empathize, an opportunity that is essential to moral development, according to the research (Kohlberg, Levin, and Hewer, 1983). Extensive research indicates that role taking and reciprocal interaction are the essential elements to children's moral development (Goldstein, 1988). Conflict resolution skills, such as perspective taking and role taking, have been found to be "central to cognitive development, moral reasoning, social intelligence [and] cooperation" (Johnson and Johnson, 1979, p. 54).

Review of the Literature

Conflict resolution program evaluations show that such programs not only reduce aggression and violence in communities and their schools but also provide "life-long decision-making skills" (U.S. Department of Justice, 1997, p. 55). A study conducted by the Center for Law-Related Education (Bodine, 1996) found that most conflict resolution programs reduce the time teachers spent on conflicts, improve school climate, and enhance problem-solving skills and self-control among students.

Studies of conflict resolution programs often demonstrate positive changes in the classroom or school climate (Jones, 1998a). Although conflict resolution programs that engage the entire school population are the most effective for improving school climate, peer mediation and conflict resolution cadre programs are also effective in improving students' ability to handle conflict and decreasing aggressive behaviors (Jones, 1998b).

There are several studies that show improved problem solving and increased cooperation as a result of successful conflict resolution programs (Crawford and Bodine, 1996; Heydenberk and Heydenberk, 2000; Johnson and Johnson, 1996). The gains in cooperative conflict resolution skills are significant for two reasons. First, in America our "children are often so . . . inappropriately competitive that they lose the opportunity to win prizes that require even minimal cooperation" (Phinney and Rotheram, 1987, p. 208). Second, students in comprehensive conflict resolution programs often "hold fewer negative stereotypes" (Lantieri and Patti, 1996, p. 26). Again, this is not a simple effect. This anti-bias effect may be the result of improved integrative (win-win) thinking for the biased student and may also negate the minority effect for the student recipient of such bias.

A related body of research has shown that, even when controlling for intelligence differences, social competence and affect regulation are powerful predictors of competent reasoning (Wentzel, 1991). Furthermore, studies have shown that the analysis of conflict in academic settings may increase epistemic curiosity and reflection (Johnson, 1979; Johnson and Johnson, 1991). Studies have also shown that the development of moral reasoning is enhanced by an increased sense of social attachment and the ability to take the perspective of others (Piaget, 1997). Although behavioral and social outcomes of conflict resolution programs have been explored, little attention has been accorded the underlying mental processes, such as moral reasoning, which may contribute to changes in behavior.

The Conflict Resolution Classroom and Moral Reasoning

Conflict resolution pilot studies showed increased student cooperation, attachment, and prosocial behaviors, all of which are related to increased moral reasoning (Heydenberk and Heydenberk, 2000). When studying how children develop a sense of justice, Piaget (1997) tells us that reciprocity and "notion of justice" are "the direct result of cooperation" (p. 198). Piaget states that "social constraint does not really suffice to socialize the child but accentuates its egocentrism. Cooperation, on the other hand, seems to be essentially the social relation which tends to eliminate infantile phenomena" (Piaget, 1997, p. 348). A child must have opportunities to decide what is morally right rather than have a set of rules imposed on him or her arbitrarily at all times. As Kohn (1986) contends, "the more we manage students' behavior and try to make them do what we say, the more difficult it is for them to become morally sophisticated people who think for themselves and care about others" (p. 62). Kohn (1986) tells us that children who are forced to obey a rule and punished if they fail to do so without any reasoning are many times more likely to break rules when they are away from parents and teachers. Children who understand the reasoning behind a rule are more likely to obey that rule when alone. Punishment is a poor substitute for reasoning once a child is developmentally ready to reason and understand.

Conflict resolution affords opportunities for students to recognize and describe their own feelings and others'. The ability to reason and empathize may be more important than strict rule enforcement in the development of moral reasoning. Kolhberg (Kohlberg, Levine, and Hewer, 1983) tells us that "a moral atmosphere is a factor influencing the growth of individual moral judgment through the stages" (p. 59). The extent of the moral growth may depend on "the degree to which moral judgment and taking into account others' viewpoints occurred within the school and the extent to which subjects felt a sense of power and participation in making rules" (p. 59) as well as whether or not the "existing rules were perceived as fair" (p. 59). Kohlberg and his colleagues (1983) found that moral reasoning is fostered in democratic settings where students participate in the problem solving and reasoning that affects their lives.

Simply being exposed to others' perspectives may engender "a sense of moral improvement or social responsibility" (Purdie, Hattie, and Douglas, 1996, p. 94). Although Prothrow-Stith (1994) acknowledges the serious limitations of stand-alone conflict resolution programs, she finds that when students are in a cooperative conflict resolution classroom they learn "cognitive skills for reasoning, weighing consequences, and making choices. Research . . . confirms that students with superior language skills and analytic abilities are less likely to use force to persuade and more likely to use creative and intellectual exercises to imagine and respect differing viewpoints" (Prothrow-Stith, 1994, p. 11).

The relationship between cognitive development and moral reasoning has been fairly well established over decades of research (Bar-Tal, 1976; Eisenberg, 1982). How rudimentary empathy evolves into fully developed moral reasoning has also been explored. The cognitive processes requisite to developing empathy begin with a minimum degree of "self-other differentiation" (Eisenberg and Strayer, 1987, p. 90) and the "ability to role-take" (p. 90). Although empathy is generally related to prosocial behavior and moral reasoning, it does not predict such behavior (Eisenberg, 1982). In Hoffman's decades of research (1987) on the relationship between empathy and moral reasoning, he has explored many stages and types of empathy. The empathy for another's life condition "may develop in childhood" as one acquires the ability to form social concepts; "one's empathic distress may also be combined with a mental representation of the plight of an entire group or class of people. . . . This empathetic level can constitute a motive base . . . for the development of certain moral ideologies" (Eisenberg and Strayer, 1987, p. 52).

Increased understanding of others and increased empathy are the core goals and the central effects of the conflict resolution curriculum. Eisenberg and Strayer (1987) suggest that empathy precedes moral principles and prescribe a "moral education" (p. 69) that requires us to consider the context and influences on others as we consider their problems. Finally, they also prescribe a "curriculum that stresses the common humanity of all people and includes efforts to raise peoples' [sic] levels of empathy"

(Eisenberg and Strayer, 1987, p. 69), particularly for people who are not in our immediate group. Moral reasoning is often developed and applied to in-group members only. Efforts that include "face-to-face cultural contact and training in role-taking procedures" (Hoffman, 1987, p. 69) in combination with "rule systems and empathy-enhancing moral education" (p. 69) will strengthen our moral reasoning. Damon's research (1999) concludes that "interactions with peers can spur moral growth by showing children the conflict between their preconceptions and social reality . . . children who participating actively in the debate, both expressing their opinions and listening to the viewpoints of others, were especially likely to benefit" (p. 77) from increased moral reasoning.

Comprehensive conflict resolution programs afford students opportunities to consider the perspectives of others as well as reflect on their own perspectives. Research using Kohlberg's stages has shown that children who are exposed to moral reasoning discrepant from their own stage, and somewhat more advanced, will prefer the higher-level reasoning to reasoning strategies from their own stage (Staub, 1978, p. 49). Role-taking opportunities seem to facilitate a child's ability to reason morally at a higher level. Teaching moral virtue alone doesn't work without experiencing the role taking and reasoning firsthand (Staub, 1978).

Goldstein (1988) feels that in order to enhance moral reasoning at least three conditions must be met: "role-taking opportunities through reciprocal social interaction, cognitive conflict regarding genuine moral dilemmas, and exposure to the next higher stage of reasoning" (p. 292). Studies that have used authentic "real-life situations" (p. 293) to resolve conflict have shown positive effects on moral reasoning. In fact, "the most effective moral education interventions occur with discussion of real dilemmas in the context of a real group (for instance, the classroom or the family)" (p. 295). Conflicts in the classroom are rich resources for the development of student reasoning.

Because the short-term results of punishments often are that the desired change is effected, it is easy to be distracted from the body of research on the long-term results. The long-term results of punitive control instead of reasoning are that children calculate risks "figuring out when they can get away with something" (Kohn, 1990, p. 168). Another effective argument Kohn (1990) makes against punitive classroom control is that such control emphasizes the consequences to "them," the student (p. 172). In other words, the reason we shouldn't rob the bank or hurt a classmate should be that it is unethical and that it harms others, not that we could get caught or punished.

Kohn (1990) cites "listening" (p. 241) and "perspective-taking as essential to the growth of reasoning, respect, and a prosocial orientation" (p. 244). Kohn (1990) prescribes cooperative learning, respectful listening, perspective taking, class meetings, and unity building activities for our students.

There are several ways empathy develops in a child, among them affective role taking and inductive techniques, "which encourage the child to imagine that he was in the place of a person who was hurt" (Goldstein, 1988, p. 55). Although not all role taking in a cooperative "prosocial situation is effective . . . [and] role-talking practice in competitive situations may not lead to increased empathy" (p. 55), generally training in perspective taking increases empathy and understanding.

Hoffman's review (1987) of the research shows that "empathetic affect is most likely to be generated when we try to imagine how we would feel if the stimuli impinging on the other person were impinging on us" (p. 284). This "cognitive restructuring or transformation of events . . . is a [sic] subject to conscious control" (p. 284). Moral motives, dispositions, and reasoning are related to "complex cognitive processes" (p. 311). Feshbach, Feshbach, Fauvre, and Ballard-Campbell (1983) developed a model of empathy and reasoning that considers both empathy and affective and cognitive factors. The first component is a child's ability to recognize the affective states of others. The second cognitive factor is the "more advanced level of cognitive competence required to assume the perspective and role of another" (p. 320). Conflict resolution skill training directly teaches students to recognize their own and others' affective states and take another's perspective—the essential skills for moral reasoning.

Damon's moral reasoning experiments (1999) brought groups of four children at a time into the lab. The ages of children in the groups were four to six and eight to ten. Children were asked to make jewelry, for which they received chocolate bars. They were to decide among themselves how to fairly divide the reward. Damon found that children who were involved in "debates about dividing the chocolate . . . seemed to pick up new, more informed ideas about justice. . . . Peer debate had heightened their awareness of the rights of others" (p. 75). Damon believes that such discussion and interaction with peers "can spur moral growth" (p. 75).

In a conflict-positive, integrative thinking environment, special attention is given to separating people from problems ("attack the problem, not the person"), emphasizing problem solving rather than affixing blame. With anger and fear minimized in the conflict-positive classroom setting, one might expect "that in the course of a person's development empathetic affects will become meaningfully associated with moral principles" (Hoffman, 1987, p. 58). The moral principles combined with a well-developed empathic understanding might then guide an individual's moral judgment, decision making, and action (Hoffman, 1987).

Moral Reasoning and Attachment

Conflict resolution education programs often have positive effects on school attachment as a result of conflict resolution training (Heydenberk and Heydenberk, 1997a). It is essential to create "a bond between self and others" and a "caring" in order to produce "the basic components of a prosocial orientation" (Staub, 1978, p. 111). Without bonds and empathy, "moral development resembles simple rule orientation" (p. 112). Empathy and bonds are therefore the source or component of a true "principle of justice" (p. 119). Moral reasoning is fostered through "the work of the community" (Piaget, 1997, p. 354) and "attachment to the social group" (p. 354). Hawkins and his colleagues (Hawkins and others, 1992) found that increased school attachment was related to students' "belief in the moral order" (p. 150) and to the students' consideration of others' feelings and the consequences of their actions. Students' communication skills improve in schools that have effective conflict resolution programs in place (Johnson and Johnson, 1995a, 1996). The improved communication and conflict resolution skills help students form prosocial bonds or attachments (Hawkins, 1995). When aggressive students learn conflict resolution skills and skills that allow them to increase positive social interaction, they often begin to prefer to form attachment bonds with prosocial and less "deviant" friends (Gilmore, Hawkins, Day, and Catalano, 1992, p. 83).

The research on resilience in children shows that strong attachments are perhaps the most important protective factor for a child in any environment (Resnick and others, 1997; Farrington and others, 1990; Baruch and Stutman, 1993; Hawkins, 1995). Poor affect regulation, poor social skills, and deficits in social cue reading often predict peer rejection, weak attachments, and alienation. "Resolving conflicts in principled ways promotes and preserves relationships thereby facilitating the bonding that is essential" (Crawford and Bodine, 1996, p. 73). Without a conflict resolution program, conflicts can predict "detachment from school and lower grades" (Johnson and Johnson, 1996, p. 482). Within a cooperative conflict resolution program, students are empowered to create friendships and broadened perspectives of their community. David Hawkins summarizes it well: "Not only does better communication address the risk factor of antisocial behavior, but one also presumes that people who can communicate well can more easily form bonds with others than people who can't" (Catalano and others, 1993, p. 15).

The American Psychological Association (APA) Commission on Violence and Youth (Eron, Gentry, and Schlegel, 1994) suggests that schools provide a unique opportunity to "create positive connections across group lines" (p. 307). Among the APA task force recommendations (Eron, Gentry, and Schlegel, 1994) are "the development of cognitive and interpersonal skills for conflict resolution" (p. 89) rather than the "heavy and inflexible use of school rules" (p. 41) that lead to increased student alienation and aggression. Elias and others (1997) state that "an emotional attachment to teachers, peers, and school is a vital link to academic success" (p. 45). They suggest that emotional literacy, cooperative learning, active "listening to others, taking others' points of view, negotiating, and using the generic steps of problem solving" (p. 55) can build prosocial attachment, helping students "reach an original resolution that is internally satisfying" (p. 60) when faced with conflict.

The research shows that once students have learned peaceful, constructive ways to resolve conflicts they embrace the integrative thinking in school and on the streets (Johnson and Johnson, 1996; Heydenberk and Heydenberk, 2000). The conflict resolution classroom may give students many of the tools they need to realize their common humanity.

Purpose of the Study

The purpose of this study was to investigate changes in students' dispositions toward moral reasoning as a result of their placement in a comprehensive conflict resolution program. The hypothesis was this: conflict resolution skill development will positively affect students' moral reasoning.

Design of the Study

This study employed a pretest-posttest comparison group design. Intact classrooms were used, reducing the threat of reactive arrangements. The design controlled for "the main effects of history, maturation, testing and instrumentation" (Campbell and Stanley, 1963, p. 48). Each year, groups were pretested early in the school year and posttested in May and early June. The Students' Attitude About Conflict (SAAC) scale and the Dispositions Toward Moral Reasoning (DMR) scale served as criterion measures. All items on the SAAC and the DMR were read aloud to students by the researcher to accommodate a range of reading and oral vocabulary abilities within the classes. Questions regarding vocabulary were entertained by the examiner to ensure intelligent responses to items. All student responses were anonymous; therefore group means were obtained for comparison purposes. The classroom teachers were in the room during the administration of the instruments to provide student assistance when indicated.

Sample

The study employed ten treatment and eight comparison groups. The sample comprised fourth- and fifth-grade students from a suburban Philadelphia school district and from the Philadelphia School District. Neither group had conflict resolution or peer mediation programs prior to Project Peace implementation. The suburban school district has approximately 520 elementary students in two schools. The majority of the students are from lower-middle-class families. The demographics for the suburban district show the population to be 65 percent Caucasian, 30 percent African American, and 5 percent designated as "other." However, because a disproportionate percentage of Caucasian students attend the local parochial school, our public school sample is 50 percent African American and 50 percent Caucasian.

The Philadelphia school under investigation had a high rate of violence and unemployment relative to other Philadelphia neighborhoods. The sample was drawn from one elementary school that serves approximately five hundred kindergarten through fifth-grade students, approximately 90 percent of whom are African American and 10 percent of whom are Hispanic, Caucasian, or Asian. With few exceptions, the students in the Philadelphia school sample qualified for the free lunch program.

All of the students in the treatment classrooms were fourth-grade students whose teachers had participated in the Peace Center's training, called Project Peace. Although younger students were included in the conflict resolution program, they were not included in the study because of the difficulty level of the criterion instruments. The Philadelphia comparison group teacher was chosen because she was not employed within the district at the time of the Project Peace training. Likewise, the two teachers from the suburban school comparison group were unavailable for training because of personal reasons (a medical leave and family business). The suburban Philadelphia comparison group consisted of two fifth-grade classrooms. All teachers volunteered to participate in the study. There were no significant differences between any of the classrooms (two treatment and one comparison classroom group in Philadelphia, two treatment and two comparison groups in the suburban school) on any of the measures at the time of the pretest. Each of the seven teachers in the study had between twenty-four and thirty-one years of teaching experience. Through questionnaires and observations, it was determined that the teachers generally employed similar teaching methods in all classrooms in each of the two schools.

The Treatment

The Project Peace treatment is a comprehensive, integrated conflict resolution program that focuses on teacher training. Project Peace teachers received approximately twelve hours of conflict resolution in-service training conducted over several days and extensive support for integrating conflict resolution skills in the classroom environment. The Project Peace in-service was followed by weekly or biweekly support meetings facilitated by Peace Center trainers for the teachers. Project Peace classroom strategies included class meetings, conflict resolution centers, use of *I* statements, active listening strategies, paraphrasing techniques, peer mediation training for students, and the development of affective vocabulary through the check-in activities. The check-in enabled each student to develop affective vocabulary through the use of modified *I* statements at the beginning of the school day. Conflict positive communication was emphasized, and the use of *I* statements was encouraged in cooperative learning groups throughout the school day. Students were taught to use conflict resolution centers, and they expanded their affective vocabulary in group settings such as class meetings, in the context of content learning, and in their journal writing.

Program implementation was confirmed through the administration of the SAAC scale, a standardized instrument. The level of implementation was monitored by Peace Center staff, and teacher feedback was considered as well. Two classrooms were eliminated during the pilot study because of evidence of low program implementation. For instance, students in these classes could not describe the steps of conflict resolution at the time of the posttest, and they knew little about class meetings.

Instruments

Two instruments were used in the study. The first was a modified form of the Students' Attitudes About Conflict scale (SAAC) by Jenkins and Smith (1992). This test was used to verify implementation of conflict resolution strategies in the classroom (the independent variable in the study). Developed by the New Mexico Center for Dispute Resolution to measure the effects of a statewide conflict resolution education initiative, the SAAC comprises thirty-two items that were selected after determining their reliability. This study involved twelve hundred fourth through twelfth-grade students in New Mexico public schools during the 1986–87 school year. The item-total correlations were examined, and items with values less than .20 were discarded, resulting in the final version of thirty-two items. Factor analytic procedures were used to assess the construct validity of the SAAC. As a result of the factor analytic procedures, four underlying factors corresponding to four clusters of items were identified. These underlying factors were labeled as the four subscales of this instrument. The four subscales that were identified by the test developers are related to school attachment, conflict resolution skills, peer relationships, and social skills.

A yes-no response format was substituted for the four-point Likert scale because the scale was considered by the researchers to be too difficult for some members of the sample of elementary students used in this study, particularly those for whom English was a second language. The decision to adopt the yes-no format was predicated upon several years of administering the SAAC to classes of students who share attributes similar to those of the sample employed in this study.

The ten items that make up the Dispositions Toward Moral Reasoning scale were designed to be consistent with Kohlberg's definition of moral reasoning, which embodies the universal principles of justice, equality, reciprocity, and respect for human rights. The items were inspired by teacher observations and comments pertaining to students' treatment of each other during the two-year pilot study in Philadelphia. All ten items reflect Kohlberg's definition and were designed to assess a sense of justice, respect, and reciprocity:

I try to treat others as I would like them to treat me.
I'm a fair person and people can always trust me.
I often go along with my friends even when I think what they are doing is wrong.

Treatment of the Data

Anonymity was required by both school districts participating in this study. Therefore, the student scores were combined to obtain a mean pretest and posttest score on each of the two instruments used in this study. Group means were obtained for two fourth-grade treatment classrooms and one fourth-grade comparison classroom in the Philadelphia School District over a period of two years. Over a three-year period, group means were obtained for two fourth-grade treatment classrooms and two fifth-grade comparison classrooms in two suburban Philadelphia schools. A single tailed t-test was used to determine significant differences between the group pretest means and group posttest means on moral reasoning. The SAAC was used to assess increases in school attachment, peer relations, and conflict resolution skill development. The SAAC conflict resolution subscale was used to confirm Project Peace program implementation. The .05 confidence level was adopted for all measures under consideration.

Findings

The differences between SAAC pretest and posttest scores confirmed conflict resolution program implementation in conflict resolution treatment classrooms. The SAAC score changes in treatment classrooms were significant at the .05 level. No significant changes in the SAAC scores were found in any of the comparison classrooms. The differences can be seen in Table 1 and Figures 1 and 2. The hypothesis (conflict resolution skill development will increase students' moral reasoning) was pretested and posttested using the DMR in the treatment and comparison classrooms. Significant changes between pretest and posttest moral reasoning scale measures were found in all treatment classrooms. Using the single tailed t-test with an alpha .05 level of significance, no changes were found

Table 1. Students' Attitudes About Conflict (SAAC) Scale Scores

	Pretest	Standard Deviation	Posttest	Standard Deviation	t Score
Treatment group	19.460	1.633	24.568	2.819	9.988*
N =	10				
Comparison group	20.481	2.288	19.805	.968	0.699
N =	8				

Note: *$p < .05$.

Figure 1. Ten Treatment Groups' Mean Pretest and Posttest SAAC Scores

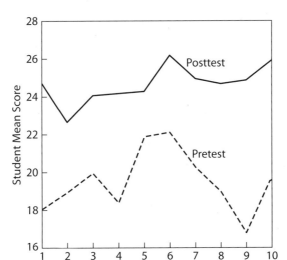

Figure 2. Eight Comparison Groups' Mean Pretest and Posttest SAAC Scores

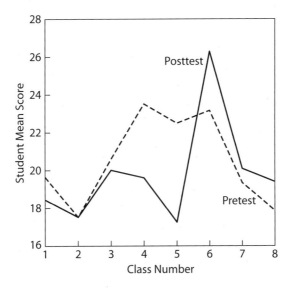

in any of the comparison classrooms, as shown in Table 2 and Figures 3 and 4.

All treatment classrooms in the study showed significant gains on the moral reasoning scale (DMR). No gains were found on the scale in the comparison classrooms. Therefore the hypothesis was accepted.

Table 2. Dispositions Toward Moral Reasoning (DMR) Scale Scores

	Pretest	Standard Deviation	Posttest	Standard Deviation	t Score
Treatment group	5.493	.375	7.831	1.063	10.032*
N =	10				
Comparison group	5.649	.667	5.657	1.114	0.025
N =	8				

Note: $*p < .05.$

Figure 3. Ten Treatment Groups' Mean Pretest and Posttest Moral Reasoning Scale Scores

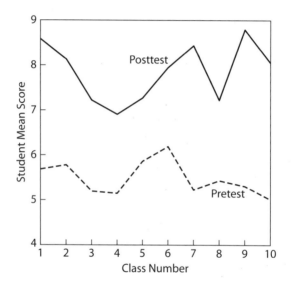

Summary, Conclusions, and Recommendations

The purpose of this study was to investigate the effect of conflict resolution training on students' moral reasoning. Most studies on conflict resolution programs focus on changes in aggressive or disruptive school behaviors. This study was inspired by pilot research that found increases in cooperation, school attachment, and prosocial behavior as a result of conflict resolution training. According to previous research, these constructs are precursors, or are associated with, moral reasoning. Several correlates of moral reasoning (such as empathy and cooperation) are theoretically posited, but for the most part they lack validation.

Figure 4. Eight Comparison Groups' Mean Pretest and Posttest Moral Reasoning Scale Scores

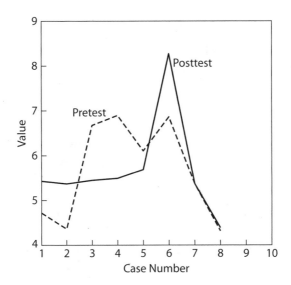

The question of how moral reasoning, the cognitive underpinning of behavioral changes, might be directly affected by conflict resolution and peer mediation strategies has received little attention from researchers. If moral reasoning can be elevated, there is hope that positive outcomes of conflict resolution training would transcend the specific rule-prescribed behavioral changes made within the school setting. Theoretically, increased moral reasoning would empower students to change behavior and social interactions in all facets of life.

This study found conflict resolution training to have positive effects on students' moral reasoning. Unlike the changes in specific school-related behaviors attributable to conflict resolution programs, moral reasoning is a cognitive function engaging higher-order thinking; it is the underpinning or determinant of behavioral choices and values. Apparently the conflict resolution training cultivated higher-order thinking processes that inspire the social and moral development of the individual. Furthermore, evidence that indicates student use of conflict resolution strategies outside of the school environment demonstrates influence beyond mere rule orientation within a prescribed setting to that of generalized increased reasoning in varied contexts (Heydenberk and Heydenberk 1998a, 1998b).

The positive findings of this study justify the time and cost associated with providing conflict resolution skills in our schools. This validation is important in the current educational climate in which the cognitive domain (academic achievement) is ranked far above the affective domain of the learner. To retain a place in the school day, programs such as conflict resolution—which are considered curricular extras—must clearly demonstrate their contribution to student reasoning. Without such evidence, conflict resolution programs risk being eliminated. The behavioral changes of students, established by many previous studies, along with the complementary evidence of improved moral reasoning brought about by conflict resolution programs should help ensure a place for conflict resolution programs within our schools.

References

Bar-Tal, D. *Prosocial Behavior.* Washington, D.C.: Hemisphere, 1976.

Baruch, R., and Stutman, S. "Strategies for Fostering Resilience." Paper presented at the World Mental Health Federation Conference, Institute for Mental Health Initiatives, Washington, D.C., Aug. 25, 1993.

Bodine, R. "From Peer Mediation to Peaceable Schools." *Update on Law-Related Education,* 1996, *20* (2), 7–9.

Campbell, D., and Stanley, J. *Experimental and Quasi-Experimental Designs for Research.* Boston: Houghton Mifflin, 1963.

Catalano, R., Hawkins, D., Herman, E., Ransdell, M., Roberts, C., Roden, T., and Starkman, N. *Preventing Violence: A Framework for Schools and Communities.* Seattle: Developmental Research Program, 1993.

Crawford, D., and Bodine, R. *Conflict Resolution Education: A Guide to Implementing Programs in Schools, Youth-Serving Organizations, and Community and Juvenile Justice Settings.* Washington, D.C.: Department of Justice, 1996.

Damon, W. "The Moral Development of Children." *Scientific American,* 1999, *2,* 72–78.

Eisenberg, N. *The Development of Prosocial Behavior.* New York: Academic Press, 1982.

Eisenberg, N., and Strayer, J. *Empathy and Its Development.* Cambridge, Mass.: Cambridge University Press, 1987.

Elias, M. J., Zins, J. E., Weissberg, R. P., Frey, K. S., Greenberg, M. T., Haynes, N. M., Kessler, R., Schwab-Stone, M. E., and Shriver, T. P. *Promoting Social and Emotional Learning: Guidelines for Educators.* Alexandria, Va.: Association for Supervision and Curriculum Development, 1997.

Eron, L., Gentry, J., and Schlegel, P. *Reason to Hope: A Psychological Perspective on Violence and Youth.* Washington, D.C.: American Psychological Association, 1994.

Farrington, D. P., Loeber, R., Elliot, D. S., Hawkins, D. J., Kandel, D. B., Klein, M. W., McCord, J., Rowe, D. C., and Tremblay, R. E. "Advancing Knowledge About the Onset of Delinquency and Crime." In B. B. Lahey and A. E. Kazdin (eds.), *Advances in Clinical Child Psychology, Vol. 13*. New York: Plenum, 1990.

Feshbach, N. D., Feshbach, S., Fauvre, M., and Ballard-Campbell, M. *Learning to Care*. Glenview, Ill.: Scott, Foresman, 1983.

Gilmore, M., Hawkins, J. D., Day, E. L., and Catalano, R. "Friendship and Deviance: New Evidence on an Old Controversy." *Journal of Early Adolescence*, Feb. 1992, pp. 80–95.

Goldstein, A. P. *The Prepare Curriculum*. Champaign, Ill.: Research Press, 1988.

Haggerty, R. J., Sherrod, L. R., Garmey, N., and Rutter, M. "Stress, Risk, and Resilience in Children and Adolescents: Process, Mechanisms, and Interventions." In R. J. Haggerty (ed.), *Social Competence*. Cambridge, England: Cambridge University Press, 1994.

Hawkins, D. J. "Controlling Crime Before It Happens." *National Institute of Justice Journal*, Aug. 1995, pp. 10–18.

Hawkins, D. J., Catalono, R. F., Morrison, D. M., O'Donnell, J., Abbott, R. D., and Day, L. E. "The Seattle Social Development Project: Effects of the First Four Years on Protective Factors and Problem Behaviors." In J. McCord and R. Tremblay (eds.), *The Prevention of Anti-Social Behavior in Children*. New York: Guilford Press, 1992.

Heydenberk, W. R., and Heydenberk, R. A. "Conflict Positive Classrooms in At-Risk Schools." Paper presented at the World Peace Organization 50th Anniversary of the U.N. Conference, New York, Oct. 27, 1997a.

Heydenberk, W. R., and Heydenberk, R. A. "Creating Metacognitive Listeners." Paper presented at the 33rd Annual Bloomsburg University Reading Conference, Bloomsburg, Pa., May 6, 1997b.

Heydenberk, W. R., and Heydenberk, R. A. "Building Bridges from the Classroom Out." Paper presented at the 13th Annual National Institute of Dispute Resolution Conference, Columbus, Ohio, July 12, 1998a.

Heydenberk, W. R., and Heydenberk, R. A. "Creating Conflict Positive Schools." Paper presented to the Pennsylvania State House of Representatives Subcommittee on Violence in Schools, Philadelphia, Sept. 8, 1998b.

Heydenberk, W. R., and Heydenberk, R. A. *A Powerful Peace: The Integrative Thinking Classroom*. Boston: Allyn and Bacon, 2000.

Hoffman, M. "The Contribution of Empathy to Justice and Moral Judgment." In N. Eisenberg and J. Strayer (eds.), *Empathy and Its Development*. New York: Cambridge University Press, 1987.

Jenkins, J., and Smith, M. "Mediation in the Schools—Program Evaluation." Albuquerque: New Mexico Center for Dispute Resolution, 1992.

Johnson, D. W. "Type of Task and Student Achievement, and Attitudes in Interpersonal Cooperation, Competition and Individualization." *Journal of Social Psychology*, 1979, *108*, 37–48.

Johnson, D. W., and Johnson, R. T. "Conflict in the Classroom: Controversy and Learning." *Review of Educational Research*, 1979, *49* (1), 51–70.

Johnson, D., and Johnson, R. "Collaboration and Cognition." In A. Costa (ed.), *Developing Minds: A Resource Book for Teaching Thinking*. Alexandria, Va.: ASCD, 1991.

Johnson, D., and Johnson, R. T. *Reducing School Violence Through Conflict Resolution*. Alexandria, Va.: American Association of Supervision and Curriculum Development, 1995a.

Johnson, D., and Johnson, R. T. "Teaching Students to Be Peacemakers: Results of Five Years of Research." *Journal of Peace Psychology,* 1995b, *1,* 417–438.

Johnson, D., and Johnson, R. T. "Why Violence Prevention Programs Don't Work—and What Does." *Educational Leadership,* 1995c, *52* (5), 63–68.

Johnson, D., and Johnson, R. T. "Conflict Resolution and Peer Mediation Programs in Elementary and Secondary Schools: A Review of the Research." *Review of Educational Research,* 1996, *66* (4), 459–506.

Jones, T. "The Comprehensive Peer Mediation Evaluation Project: Insights and Directions for Curriculum Integration." *Forum,* 1998a, *6* (35), 9–12.

Jones, T. "Research Supports Effectiveness of Peer Mediation." *The Fourth R,* Mar.-Apr. 1998b, *82* (1), 1–25.

Kohlberg, L., Levine, C., and Hewer, A. *Moral Stages: A Current Formulation and a Response to Critics.* Basel, Switzerland: Karger, 1983.

Kohn, A. *No Contest: The Case Against Competition.* Boston: Houghton Mifflin, 1986.

Kohn, A. *The Brighter Side of Human Nature: Altruism and Empathy in Everyday Life.* New York: Basic Books, 1990.

Lantieri, L., and Patti, J. "The Road to Peace in Our Schools." *Educational Leadership,* 1996, *54* (1), 28–31.

Nemecek, S. "In Focus: Forestalling Violence." *Scientific American,* 1998, *9* (7), 15–16.

Phinney, J., and Rotheram, M. J. *Children's Ethnic Socialization: Pluralism and Development.* Thousand Oaks, Calif.: Sage, 1987.

Piaget, J. *The Moral Judgment of the Child.* New York: Free Press, 1997.

Prothrow-Stith, D. "Building Violence Prevention into the Curriculum." *School Administrator,* Apr. 1994, pp. 8–12.

Purdie, N., Hattie, J., and Douglas, G. "Students' Conceptions of Learning and Their Use of Self-Regulated Learning Strategies: A Cross-Cultural Comparison." *Journal of Educational Psychology,* 1996, *88* (1), 87–100.

Resnick, M. D., Bearman, P. S., Blum, R. W., Bauman, K. E., Harris, K. M., Jones, J., Tabor, J., Beuhring, T., Sieving, R. E., Shew, M., Ireland, M., Bearinger, L. H., and Udry, J. R. "Protecting Adolescents from Harm: Findings from the National Longitudinal Study on Adolescent Health." *Journal of the American Medical Association,* 1997, *278* (10), 823–832.

Staub, E. *Positive Social Behavior and Morality.* New York: Academic Press, 1978.

U.S. Department of Justice. *Conflict Resolution,* Mar. 1997, p. 55.

Wentzel, K. R. "Relations Between Social Competence and Academic Achievement in Early Adolescence." *Child Development,* 1991, *62,* 1066–1078.

Warren R. Heydenberk is a faculty member at Lehigh University. He has taught in elementary through adult levels in public schools and in alternative education settings.

Roberta Anna Heydenberk is an adjunct faculty member at Lehigh University, where she has taught multicultural education and conflict resolution courses. She has more than a decade of service in conflict resolution program research and curriculum design. The Heydenberks are recipients of numerous awards, and they serve on national and international education boards. They are authors of *A Powerful Peace: The Integrative Thinking Classroom* and *When I Get Angry.*

Sharon Perkins Bailey serves as program director of the National Conference on Peacemaking and Conflict Resolution (NCPCR). Along with John A. Bachnowicz, she served as trainer-facilitator of Project Peace during the time of this study.

Mediator Mentors: Improving School Climate, Nurturing Student Disposition

PAMELA S. LANE-GARON

TIM RICHARDSON

Mediator Mentors, a collaborative research and service project, was begun by California State University-Fresno faculty and the staff of an elementary school (K–8) in the Central San Joaquin Valley. The purpose of the research was to assess conflict resolution program effects on students (N = 300) and school climate. Cross-age mentoring is an important component of this collaborative project. University students preparing for roles in helping professions served as mentors to elementary students. Impacts on student cognitive and affective perspective taking were assessed and student perceptions of school safety were explored.

Education is in the midst of an essentialist movement, with academic achievement and accountability our primary foci. All empirical and anecdotal evidence tells us that the pursuit of academic achievement requires learning environments that foster civility, safety, and connectedness. Mediator Mentors, a collaborative research and service project, was begun by California State University-Fresno faculty and the staff of Herndon-Barstow Elementary School (K–8) in the Central San Joaquin Valley in July 2000. The purpose of the project and research was to develop a conflict resolution program that "fit in with the life of the school" and evaluate program effects on students (N = 300) and school climate.

Herndon-Barstow had been identified as an "underperforming school" through the governor's Immediate Intervention Program (IIUSP) grant. Because of the school's history as an "overflow" enrollment site for the district, students reportedly had little identification with Herndon-Barstow and leadership noted a lack of cohesive spirit among students enrolled in the four separate attendance tracks (Herndon-Barstow is a year-round school). Focus areas and goals were designated; one of them was school climate.

Following needs assessment in August 2000, administration, a team of seven Herndon-Barstow teachers, and two CSUF professors committed themselves to peer mediation program development and evaluation. Initial needs assessment revealed that 90 percent of the staff felt a conflict management program would unite the school around a model in which listening to and appreciating divergent perspectives was inherent. Additionally, the IIUSP process indicated that "feelings of connectedness, and perceptions of safety" required improvement.

Cross-age mentoring is an essential part of the project. University student interns from California State University's Peace and Conflict Studies certificate program elected to spend 150 hours a semester mentoring Herndon-Barstow mediators.

Additionally, after similar training, teacher credential candidates also elected to mentor elementary conflict managers. These mediator mentors learn mediation skills in their college experience and with that background work weekly with elementary students trained as peer mediators.

Mediator Mentors represents an ongoing collaboration between a university and an elementary school. In its third year, the program is thriving; more than 150 students have been trained in communication, conflict resolution, and facilitation skills. The peer mediation program now has a regular influx of university students each semester. It is notable that more than half of those who mentor plan to become teachers, and the rest—counselors and social workers. The program continues to evolve with these components developed thus far:

- Assessment protocol (Davis Scales, conflict survey, standardized test scores, and school climate surveys)
- In-service of classified and certified staff (teachers, instructional assistants, playground personnel, and administrators)
- Nomination and training of cadres (across tracks) of peer mediators (grades four through eight)
- Ongoing development for identified mediators in weekly "skill spots"
- Schoolwide classroom instruction by peer mediators in conflict resolution strategies
- Cross-age mentoring (mediator mentor CSUF professors, Herndon-Barstow teachers, and university student mediator mentors; also Herndon-Barstow intermediate grade peer mediators)

- Intermediate student mentoring of primary student conflict resolution skills using literature sharing and discussion
- Local partnership schools identified (Kastner Intermediate "conflict managers" and Central High School "peer connectors")
- School climate town hall (format for school climate evaluation)
- Reward field trips for student mediators and university mentors
- School policy developed for mediator selection and maintenance in the program
- New student peer mediator welcome protocol

It was expected that after one academic year of program development (a ten-month assessment interval):

- Student cognitive and affective (empathy) perspective taking will increase in program participants, with peer mediators scoring higher on developmental assessment measures than nonmediators.
- There will be a relationship among peer mediation program implementation, standardized score increase (especially language arts), and perception of school climate for program participants.

Relevant Literature

In the American Medical Association's 1996 longitudinal study on protecting our children from harm, "connectedness with school" was found to be a factor protective against a variety of risk behaviors (violence being one). Mediator Mentors provides an ideal structure for connectedness. "Connectedness with school" can, in many cases, be translated to perceived peer acceptance (Garbarino, 1999). Students who have been helped by a peer appreciate the helper and the process (Johnson and Johnson, 1999).

The use of cross-age mentors has been thoroughly researched and is considered an effective structure supportive of interpersonal learning (Johnson and Johnson, 1999; Lieberman, 1989; McLaughlin and Hazouri, 1992). Lev Vygotsky's notion (1987) of learning in the context of interaction with the more capable peer is a sound theoretical basis for mentoring programs.

Research on effective models tells us that for the learner to accept the model's message, there must be some degree of perceived similarity, esteem, competence, and novelty. The university students interested in helping professions satisfy these criteria for the younger mediators.

Previous research on school-based mediation programs indicates that training only a small number of mediators does not prevent violence (Johnson and Johnson, 1998). However, there is evidence that as the number of trained mediators grows in proportion to the student population, school climate effects are more likely (Lane-Garon, 1998).

The Mediator Mentors project incorporates developmental considerations, school climate concerns, and influences of mentoring. Mediation's contribution to violence prevention lies in its reduction of the predictors of violence (poor communication, impulsivity, egocentrism, perceived isolation). Mediation's contribution to adaptive child development lies in its provision of a model for considering another's diverging point of view, accurately inferring another's feelings, cooperatively resolving a shared problem, and experiencing satisfaction with a mutually designed solution. Being a mediator mentor means that a young person has mastered (at his or her current developmental level) a set of communication skills, can use them in real and sometimes emotionally charged situations, and can guide others in their development of these same skills.

There are many components of successful, school-based violence prevention. The better programs (such as L. Stevahn and colleagues' kindergarten project; Stevahn, Oberlie, Johnson, and Johnson, 2000) consider child development and fit into the curriculum and life of the school. The Herndon-Barstow project, Mediator Mentors, fits easily into recess periods when conflicts are resolved on the playground as they occur. Also, intermediate peer mediators facilitate classroom instruction in the form of cross-age tutoring. When peer mediators teach a "lesson" in primary grades, they select a literature book in advance that is appropriate to their younger audience. When they visit the primary class with a partner, they read the story and discuss literature-based themes of conflict and resolution with the younger children. Lessons are short and fit into the school focus on addressing language arts and reading standards. In fact, school staff working with the mediation program have circulated a list of standards (Exhibit 1) to assist primary teachers in documenting objectives addressed by visiting mediators in their classes.

Many violence prevention programs do not consider child development, and many prevention programs do not consider the strength of mentoring relationships. Mediator Mentors combines the strengths of multiple, proven approaches: social skill development (Spivak and Shure, 1974; Garbarino, 1999), peer mediation (Marvel, Moreda, and Cook, 1993; Johnson and Johnson, 1998; Lane-Garon, 1998), and mentoring programs. The resulting gestalt is a practical program that supports a positive learning environment.

Exhibit 1. Primary Grades California Language Arts Standards Addressed by Peer Mediation Process

K.0	Listening and Speaking Strategies
	1.1 Understand and follow one- and two-step oral directions.
	1.2 Share information and ideas, speaking audibly in complete sentences.
1.0	1.1 Listen attentively.
	1.2 Ask questions for clarification and understanding.
	1.3 Give, restate, and follow simple directions.
	1.4 Stay on topic when speaking.
	1.5 Use descriptive words when speaking about people, places, things, events.
2.0	Speaking Applications
	2.1 Recount experiences or present stories that move through logical sequence of events (retell an important life event or personal experience using sequencing, and provide descriptions with careful attention to sensory detail).
3.0	Listening and Speaking
	1.1 Retell, paraphrase, and explain what has been said by a speaker.
	1.2 Connect and relate prior experiences, insights, and ideas to speaker's.
	1.3 Respond to questions with appropriate elaboration.
	1.7 Use clear and specific vocabulary to establish tone.

Peer mediation research has most often been focused on reducing incidents of physical assault and student suspension. However, Herndon-Barstow had no problem with assault, and suspension rates were relatively low (*California Safe Schools Assessment,* 1999). The school was interested in the developmental effects of program implementation on student disposition to consider the thoughts and feelings of others. Therefore developmental variables as well as contextual ones were included in the assessment protocol. Additionally, administration was interested in possible program relationship to academic performance as measured by SAT-9 scores.

Setting Specifics

Herndon-Barstow is located in a rural setting in the northwest area of Fresno County and is considered a multicommunity, year-round school. Although the school itself is in a rural setting, the majority of students come from all over the Central Unified School District, because of the school's "overflow" status. Central Unified, once a small rural district, is now the second fastest-growing district in the state, with 93 percent of the students living inside Fresno city limits. California's Central Valley is primarily agricultural and multicultural. Approximately 745 students attended Herndon-Barstow at the time the study was completed (as of March 2002, enrollment had increased to 817). In grades K–8 there are four tracks. Preschool and county special education programs are also housed on campus. Ninety-five percent of the students are bused to and from school. Seventy-eight percent of students qualify for free or reduced breakfast and lunch. The multicultural student population is approximately 28.7 percent white, 13.3 percent black, 46.6 percent Hispanic, 7 percent Filipino, .9 percent American Indian, and 9.8 percent Asian. Nineteen percent of the students are limited English proficient, with most of those having migrant status. Approximately 70 percent of the student population qualifies for Title I services on the basis of multiple measurements.

After Herndon-Barstow was identified as an "underperforming school," an intense school improvement process was begun. In conjunction with the Pulliam Group, Herndon-Barstow developed an action plan with six focus areas. The school is now in its third year of the IIUSP process. The identified foci were (1) reading achievement, (2) assessment, (3) extended learning opportunities, (4) mathematics achievement, (5) English language deficient (ELD) student transition to English language proficiency, and (6) learning environment.

Components of the Positive Learning Environment

Despite having been an overflow school for district enrollment, Herndon-Barstow also has had a strong school culture. Its evolution from a small, country school to a school with four tracks and a large, multicultural population took place rather quickly with the growth of the surrounding community. In order to maintain the character and climate it valued, Herndon-Barstow took some important steps. The school was the first in the district to outlaw sports- and gang-related clothing. The Herndon-Barstow school climate is affected by transience. Student movement increased with the multitrack, year-round schedule. The mobility rate is 68 percent. Teachers connect the rise in the number of classroom disruptions and lack of parental involvement to the high number of students entering and exiting classrooms. "Connectedness" and "team spirit" are difficult to maintain under these conditions. Classroom behavior norms need to be constantly redefined and reestablished. As a result of peer mediation program implementation, students have now taken on the role of welcoming new students to the campus and orienting them as to how "problems are solved at our school." This has reportedly increased school pride and cohesion. Since the peer mediation program is implemented across tracks, it directly affects cohesion issues.

Method

As part of the school improvement effort, elementary school administration sought peer mediation program development to improve student perceptions of safety and connectedness, and ultimately to affect academic performance. Ninety percent of staff were interested in engaging in mediation program development. Seven staff members received training and worked collaboratively to train elementary students. Classified personnel were also trained in order that their own, necessary roles on the playground would interface easily and supportively with the new peer mediators. First, however, university-conducted assessments were completed previous to peer mediation training. A blanket assessment of student cognitive, affective, and contextual variables was administered to participants in grades four through eight. Importantly, mediators and non-mediators were not yet distinguished at the time of the preassessment.

Measurement Protocol and Instrument Description

The Davis Scales of the Interpersonal Reactivity Index have been used in previous studies of mediation and social skills training interventions (Davis, 1980; Lane-Garon, 1998). On this questionnaire, respondents circled the numbers from 1 to 7 (*never* to *always*) to indicate self-perceptions of their dispositional perspective taking. For example, item four on the cognitive reads, "I believe there are two sides to every question and try to look at them both." A rating of 7 would indicate a strong dispositional tendency to consider differing perspectives. Item three on the affective scale reads, "Other people's misfortunes do not usually disturb me a great deal." A rating of 7 of this reverse-scored item would indicate a low level of empathy or affective perspective taking. Davis reported Cronbach internal reliability alpha coefficients of .75 for males and .78 for females on the cognitive scale and .72 for males and .70 for females on the affective scale.

The Davis Scales were considered an appropriate measure for assessing social-cognitive dispositional tendency according to the assumption that cognitive and affective processes are interrelated, can be assessed independently, and should be interpreted interactively. Davis's work represents a multidimensional approach to measurement of social-cognitive, dispositional tendency. In studying the impact of conflict resolution programs on students, we are less interested in their *ability* to consider the thoughts and feelings of others and *more* interested in their *disposition* to do so. The multicultural student population required changes to the Davis Scales: addition of explanatory stories. The addition of these short illustrations may affect the reliability of the instrument, while increasing validity of the measure when used with multicultural student populations.

The Conflict Survey (Lane-Garon, 1998) was designed to yield contextual information about the participants' personal and historical experience with conflict and violence. Participants responded to nine statements using a 7-point Likert scale.

All measurements were administered at pre- and postassessment intervals (ten months). Because of the year-round nature of the school and the four attendance tracks, peer mediation trainings took place at approximately two-month intervals, increasing the cadre of student mediators to 130 at the time of the postassessment. Only students present at program inception and at year-one assessment were included in the final data analysis.

In the first three months of the program, elementary students were nominated by their teachers, peers, and selves to become peer mediators. Stipulations were that the students' grades meet the district's criteria for cocurricular participation and signatures from two staff supporters were to be obtained. Finally, family permission to participate was also secured. The selected mediators were then trained over two days (eight hours) in communication and conflict resolution skills.

Mentors

A most important component of this proposed research project involves mentoring. When peer mediators can teach their skills to others, outside the context of their service role, they ultimately become aware of how much they know and appreciate their new skills. A linkage of mentoring relationships between college student mediators and elementary school mediators is an important component of the research project design. University student mediator mentors offered:

- Support or coaching on the playground during actual mediations
- Assistance planning for schoolwide awareness of program to promote usage
- Strategic program support: scheduling, logistics, program problem solving
- Skill development (CSUF mentors plan and conduct "skill spot" experiences to strengthen and expand elementary mediation skills)
- Cooperation with elementary school staff and university faculty in planning mediation-related events

The peer mediation program's influence was magnified by the enthusiasm of staff and students. In the first year of implementation, news coverage and presentations at local and regional conferences increased program visibility. Program participants experienced reward trips to the university and to another school with a mediation program. These occasions must be reported as part of the "treatment" in this study. It is certainly possible that the halo effect influenced study results.

Results and Discussion

The following sections report results and discuss the implications for policy and practice.

Developmental Variables: Disposition to Consider the Thoughts and Feelings of Others

The first study prediction was supported by the data. Student cognitive and affective perspective taking did in fact demonstrate a pretest to posttest increase, with peer mediators scoring higher on developmental assessment measures than nonmediators. A repeated measures analysis of variance, with time as the repeated measure, revealed an effect for cognitive perspective taking as measured by the Davis subscale of the Interpersonal Reactivity Index; $F(1,149) = 11.03, p < .001$. (See Exhibits 3.2 to 3.6 at the end of the article.) The empathy or affective perspective taking scale showed a similar effect; $F(1,149) = 15.55, p < .000$. The means for the cognitive variable increased from preassessment to postassessment. An independent samples t-test revealed that although the mediator means were not significantly different from those of nonmediators at pretest (no preexisting differences), the mediator means were significantly different from the means of nonmediators at posttest; $x = 32.923$, compared to $x = 28.521$, $p < .001$. This may indicate that the practice of mediation as a facilitator has a more powerful effect than participation as a disputant.

Pearson correlations for the empathy and cognitive variables revealed stronger relationships at postassessment than at pretest. It is interesting to note that the tendency or disposition to consider the thoughts and feelings of others (cognitive perspective taking) at preassessment is only moderately related to empathy ($r = .45, p < .000$), while at the posttest (ten months later) these variables were more highly correlated at $r = .61, p < .000$. This finding may suggest that getting into the habit of (nurturing a disposition toward) making inferences about others' thoughts can lead to more accurate understanding of others' feelings and hopefully to behavior that considers them.

With respect to change over time, the empathy variable performed similarly to the cognitive variable. There was a significant effect for the score increase in affective perspective taking, again with mediators scoring significantly higher than nonmediators; $F(1,149) = 15.55, p < .000$.

Student Experience with Conflict and Strategy Choices

When the students were asked to complete the conflict survey about their personal experience, their responses were grouped into conflict-negative and conflict-positive behaviors. For example, "People I live with resolve conflict with yelling" was scored as a conflict-negative behavior. "People I live with resolve conflict by talking it out" was scored as a conflict-positive behavior. Analysis of variance revealed that student experience with conflict-positive behavior was not differentiated by mediator status at pretest. In other words, neither group indicated they had significantly more conflict-positive experiences than the other. However, by posttest, mediators indicated significantly more conflict-positive behaviors than nonmediators; $F(1,79) = 7.53, p < .007$. The means for conflict-positive behaviors at posttest were mediators $x = 15.85$ and nonmediators $x = 13.34$. This finding suggests that training and practice in peer mediation may also affect home life, or at least the student's perception of home conflict resolution style, when looking through more informed and experienced eyes (having been trained in the school-based mediation program). Relatedly, after ten months the majority of study participants preferred to resolve interpersonal problems by talking to the individual with whom they have a difference. Initially, seeking the assistance of an adult was preferred.

This shift in strategy choice may be due to the fact that study participants who are mediators as well as those who participated as disputants increased their knowledge and ability to resolve problems peacefully. The preferred strategy choice might be explained by an acquired sense of empowerment.

Perceptions of School Climate

The Central Unified School District administers a school climate survey yearly, which generates student perceptions of school safety. In the first year of the mandated school improvement process, the Pulliam Group (1999, 2001) guided the academic interventions and also administered a school climate survey. This survey had four questions, identical to those asked the previous year on the district-administered survey. All students completed the surveys. When the responses to Pulliam's Student Learning, School Culture, Expectations for Success, and Safe Environment survey were compared to the previously administered district measure, an increase in perceptions of school safety was revealed.

When responses of 2001 were compared to those generated in 1999, 66 percent of Herndon-Barstow students either agreed or strongly agreed that they felt safe on campus. This represented an increase from 56 percent in 1999. In response to the survey item "Other students treat me with respect at school," 58 percent of Herndon-Barstow students (2001) agreed or strongly agreed, as opposed to 47 percent in 1999. Those students who agreed or strongly agreed that they were responsible for helping with safety on campus were 56 percent in 2000 versus only 49 percent in 1999. Responding to the "connectedness variable," only 47 percent felt they belonged at the school in 1999. But in 2001, after initial Mediator Mentors program implementation, 58 percent of students reported feeling they belonged (Table 1).

It should be noted that the greatest gain reported from survey data is in the perceptions of school safety domain.

Mediation and Academic Performance

Also predicted was a relationship among peer mediation program implementation, standardized score increase (especially language arts), and perception of school climate for program participants. This relationship is most difficult to determine because the academic year in which Mediator Mentors was first implemented was a "banner year" for the elementary school. Intensive reading and language arts initiatives were implemented at about the same time as the peer mediation program began. As an underperforming school, there was considerable pressure to improve test scores and to do it soon. In fact, both mediators and nonmediators improved

Table 1. Pulliam Survey

Survey Item	1999 Agree or Strongly Agree	2001 Agree or Strongly Agree
I *feel safe* at school	56%	66%
Students treat me with *respect*	47%	58%
I can help with school *safety*	49%	56%
I feel like I *belong* here	47%	58%

Source: Pulliam Group, 1999, 2001.

standardized test scores at about the same rate. The mediator mean for language arts scores at pretest was $x = 37.72$ as compared with the pretest mean for nonmediators $x = 35.50$. Ten months later, the language arts mediator mean was $x = 43.00$ and the nonmediator mean was $x = 42.65$. The groups did not differ significantly over the interval, but their growth, when added to the growth of the entire school population, was highly significant. The Academic Performance Index Score for Herndon-Barstow represented the greatest gains for any school in the district in all subject areas. In California, in the year of this study, the Academic Performance Index was calculated annually from scores on the Stanford 9 series of tests. The target for improvement in the year of this study's implementation was ten points and the growth actually achieved was forty points. This was a tremendous gain for all the students at Herndon-Barstow. There was no interaction between mediator status and standardized test score. Under these conditions, it is not possible to statistically determine the extent to which the Mediator Mentors program—with its emphasis on language and reasoning skills—influenced academic performance.

Implications for Practice

The Mediator Mentors model is fairly easy to replicate. More than 60 percent of the university mentors in this project are becoming credentialed teachers; the rest, counselors and social workers. A program in which communication and problem solving is central is a fine induction to the culture of their future profession. This type of training is often lacking in teacher education programs.

Elementary students benefit from interaction with university students who are young enough to vividly remember their own recent public school experience and who themselves care about developing empathy, practicing respectful communication, and cooperation. Mediator Mentors capitalizes on positive peer power. Parents need not be alone in teaching the values and actions of civility. Schools are increasingly recognizing and accepting their role as centers of cultural socialization. Accountability is not just about test scores but also about how we are preparing youth to deal with differences—of opinion, background, and intention.

Implications for Research

Although we are appreciative of the recommendation for increased rigor in CRE program evaluation, we have some concern about the promise of classical models of positivism in educational settings. As all educational researchers know, there is an inherent confounding of influences in school settings. Consider the control group. It is still possible to find schools without CRE programs, but thankfully these schools are usually working at increasing empathy, for example through other means (leadership or diversity training). It is nearly impossible to compare effects of a "treatment" to effects generated by "the absence of that treatment." Even in the same school, a CRE program may be focusing on increasing empathy . . . along with the diversity program, the anger management program, and the "special friends" program. We believe that we must attend to the isolation of our variables, their definitions, and measurement with integrity, but to claim that trusted empirical models produce completely reliable results in school settings is to mislead. Kmitta has presented a masterful critique of the school-based research and recommendations for a future research agenda (Jones and Kmitta, 2000).

One way to approach further CRE research is to select measurement instruments aligned with the five CRE program goals. Then, with these goals on the table for all participants to reference, the creators of the educational environments should be asked, "What do you want to accomplish with this program?" "What questions would you like to answer?" There is a very good chance that an administrator's answers will differ from a teacher's and the school psychologist's will differ from the student's. For example, in the study discussed in this article, the administration had state-mandated questions to address. When this approach is taken, there will be some instruments created that have no determined reliability, though "ecological validity" may be advanced. Practitioners often say, "Year three is magic." If indeed CRE programs build momentum over time, then opportunities to determine reliability and validity of "naïve" instruments exist, assuming there is a shared commitment to measurement improvement. We would recommend use of a combination of measures and procedures (paper-and-pencil tasks in addition to town hall meetings) to assess program impact. Developmental psychology, communication, counseling, and other disciplines associated with the promotion of adaptive human development offer us a variety of reliable and valid assessments to measure change in individual student cognitive and affective dispositions with respect to CRE program implementation. These well-established measures should be relied upon.

Interprofessional collaboration seems a natural outgrowth of well-defined CRE program goals having implications for a variety of academic disciplines and practitioner purviews. We need to maintain awareness that our work is grounded in human development and that interdisciplinary responsibility is therefore implied. Further, a number of methodological approaches to evaluation may be appropriate, so long as they emerge from a theoretical context and are aligned with the CRE goals. Attention to these cautions may advance our work and ensure its longevity in the education of youth.

References

American Medical Association. *Protecting Adolescents from Harm: National Longitudinal Study.* Chicago: American Medical Association, 1996.

California Safe Schools Assessment. Sacramento: California State Department of Education, 1999.

Davis, M. "A Multidimensional Approach to Individual Differences in Empathy." Dissertation abstracted in *JSAS Catalog of Selected Documents in Psychology,* 1980, *10* (4), 84.

Davis, M. "Measuring Individual Differences in Empathy: Evidence for a Multidimensional Approach." *Journal of Personality and Social Psychology,* 1983, *44,* 113–126.

Garbarino, J. *Lost Boys: Why Our Sons Turn Violent and How We Can Save Them.* New York: Simon & Schuster, 1999.

Johnson, D. W., and Johnson, R. "Why Violence Prevention Programs Don't Work and What Does." In A. Wolfolk (ed.), *Readings in Educational Psychology.* Boston: Allyn and Bacon, 1998.

Johnson, D. W., and Johnson, R. *Learning Together and Alone: Cooperative, Competitive, and Individualistic Learning.* Boston: Allyn and Bacon, 1999.

Jones, T. S., and Kmitta, D. *Does It Work? The Case for Conflict Resolution in Our Nation's Schools.* Washington, D.C.: Conflict Resolution Education Network (now Association for Conflict Resolution), 2000.

Lane-Garon, P. "Developmental Considerations: Encouraging Perspective Taking in Student Mediators." *Mediation Quarterly,* 1998, *16* (2), 201–215.

Lane-Garon, P. "Practicing Peace: The Impact of a School-Based Conflict Resolution Program on Elementary Students." *Peace and Change: A Journal of Peace Research,* 1999, *25*(4), 467–475.

Lieberman, D. J. *Peer Counseling in the Elementary School: Promoting Personal and Academic Growth Through Positive Relationships Thereby Increasing Self-Esteem and Self-Concept.* Washington, D.C.: Institute of Education Services, U.S. Department of Education, 1989. (ERIC document no. ED 323 449)

Marvel, J., Moreda, I., and Cook, I. *Developing Conflict Resolution Skills in Students.* Atlanta: Centers for Disease Control and Prevention and Florida Department of Health and Rehabilitative Services, 1993.

McLaughlin, M. S., and Hazouri, S. P. *TLC Tutoring Leading Cooperating: Training Activities for Elementary School Students.* Washington, D.C.: Institute of Education Services, U.S. Department of Education, 1992. (ERIC document no. ED 346 400)

Pulliam Group. *School Improvement Analysis.* Fresno, Calif.: Pulliam Group, 1999, 2001.

Spivak, G., and Shure, M. B. *Social Adjustment of Young Children.* San Francisco: Jossey-Bass, 1974.

Stevahn, L., Oberlie, K., Johnson, D. W., and Johnson, R. "The Effects of Role Reversal Training and Use of Integrative Negotiation for Classroom Management on Conflict Resolution in Kindergarten." Presentation to the American Educational Research Association, Seattle, Apr. 2000.

Vygotsky, L. *Thought and Language* (A. Kozulin, trans.). Cambridge, Mass.: MIT Press, 1987.

Exhibits

Exhibit 2. Measurement Instruments

Cognitive Perspective Taking Scale (Davis subscale of the Interpersonal Reactivity Index, 1983) [with Explanatory Stories]

Administrator comments: This test has no "right" answers. Its purpose is to determine your typical or usual disposition in a variety of situations. Circle the number for each statement that describes your typical way.

Raise your hand if you have questions. Listen, then circle, then wait for me to read the next statement aloud.

Directions: Circle the number for each statement which best describes your typical way.

1. Before criticizing somebody, I try to imagine how I would feel if I were in their place.

1	2	3	4	5	6	7
never						always

Here's an example to make the meaning of the statement clearer: Imagine a classmate coming to school with a funny haircut. Do you think about how you would feel if that were your haircut before saying anything? If this is your usual way, circle a high number. If this is only sometimes your way, circle a middle number. If you rarely think like this, circle a low number.

2. If I'm sure I'm right about something, I don't waste much time listening to other people's arguments.

1	2	3	4	5	6	7
never						always

If you rarely listen to others when your mind is made up, circle a high number. If you sometimes listen, circle a middle number. If you always listen to others' arguments even when you have your mind made up, circle a low number.

(Continued)

Exhibit 2. Measurement Instruments (Continued)

3. I sometimes try to understand my friends better by imagining how things look from their perspectives.

1	2	3	4	5	6	7
never						always

No explanation needed

4. I believe that there are two sides to every question and I try to look at them both.

1	2	3	4	5	6	7
never						always

When there's a disagreement among people, do you usually try to understand each person's point of view? If you do, circle a high number. If you sometimes do, circle a middle number. If you rarely do this, circle a low number.

5. I sometimes find it difficult to see things from the "other guy's" point of view.

1	2	3	4	5	6	7
never						always

If it is usually hard for you to view things from the point of view of someone who doesn't agree with you, circle a high number. If it is sometimes hard, circle a middle number. If it is usually easy for you to consider a different point of view, circle a low number.

6. I try to look at everybody's side of a disagreement before I make a decision.

1	2	3	4	5	6	7
never						always

Imagine you are ordering pizza with three friends who like anchovies, artichokes, and olives. You have your preference too. If you usually try to understand everyone's preference and then make the order, circle a high number. If you sometimes do this, circle a middle number. If you rarely do this, circle a low number.

7. When I'm upset at someone, I usually try to "put myself in his shoes."

1	2	3	4	5	6	7
never						always

When you are angry, do you typically try to think about the other person's thoughts and feelings? If you usually do, circle a high number. If you sometimes do, circle a middle number. If you rarely think about the other person's feelings when you are upset, circle a low number.

Source: Davis, 1983. Used by permission.

Exhibit 3. Measurement Instruments: Empathy (or Affective Perspective Taking) Scale

Davis Subscale of the Interpersonal Reactivity Index, with Explanatory Stories

Administrator comments: This test has no "right" answers. Its purpose is to determine your typical or usual disposition in a variety of situations. Circle the number for each statement that describes your typical way.

Raise your hand if you have questions. Listen, then circle, then wait for me to read the next statement aloud.

Directions: Circle the number for each statement which best describes your typical way.

1. When I see someone being taken advantage of, I feel kind of protective of them.

1	2	3	4	5	6	7
never						always

Here's an example to make the meaning of the statement clearer: Imagine you see a small child on the playground being bullied by a bigger student. If you usually feel like protecting the small student, circle a high number. If you sometimes do, circle a middle number. If you rarely feel this way, circle a low number.

2. When I see someone being treated unfairly, I sometimes don't feel very much pity for them.

1	2	3	4	5	6	7
never						always

Imagine that a student has been called to the office for discipline referral. You believe others were involved in the problem, too. If you usually wouldn't feel sorry for the student in the vice principal's office, circle a high number. If you sometimes would, circle a middle number. If you usually feel badly for those referred to the vice principal's office for discipline, circle a low number.

3. I often have tender, concerned feelings for people less fortunate than I.

1	2	3	4	5	6	7
never						always

Imagine that you see an old man walking down the street in winter without shoes on. If you would usually feel concerned, circle a high number. If you sometimes would feel concerned, circle a middle number. If this would rarely bother you, circle a low number.

4. I would describe myself as a pretty soft-hearted person.

1	2	3	4	5	6	7
never						always

(*Continued*)

Exhibit 3. Measurement Instruments: Empathy (or Affective Perspective Taking)
        Scale (Continued)

"Soft-hearted" can mean compassionate. It can mean that you have quick emotional response to the pain or sorrow of others. Some cry at sad movies or books. Some take action to help others in trouble. What is your usual way? If you consider yourself typically soft-hearted, circle a high number. If you are sometimes like this, circle a middle number. If "soft-hearted" does not usually describe you, circle a low number.

5. Sometimes I don't feel very sorry for other people when they are having problems.

1	2	3	4	5	6	7
never						always

Imagine you know a person who is out of work. If this typically doesn't bother you, circle a high number. If this would sometimes make you feel sorry for the unemployed person, circle a middle number. If you usually would feel sorry for someone out of work, circle a low number.

6. Other people's misfortunes do not usually disturb me a great deal.

1	2	3	4	5	6	7
never						always

Remember the example of the man without shoes?
Imagine that you see an old man walking down the street in winter without shoes on. If you would usually not be too bothered by seeing this, circle a high number. If you sometimes would feel concerned, circle a middle number. If you are typically disturbed by the misfortunes of others, circle a low number.

7. I am often quite touched by things that I see happen.

1	2	3	4	5	6	7
never						always

If you usually experience emotions resulting from things that you see in real life, on TV, and read in books, circle a high number. If you sometimes do, circle a middle number. If you rarely have these feelings, circle a low number.

Scoring note: Cognitive Scale reverse scored questions are numbers 2 and 5. Affective
        (Empathy) Scale reverse scored questions are numbers 2, 5, and 6.

Source: Davis, 1983. Used by permission.

Exhibit 4. Conflict Survey

1.   The people I live with resolve conflict by *talking it out.*

1	2	3	4	5	6	7
not much			some			a lot

2.   The people I live with resolve conflict by *yelling.*

1	2	3	4	5	6	7
not much			some			a lot

3.   The people I live with resolve conflict with *hitting.*

1	2	3	4	5	6	7
not much			some			a lot

4.   The people I live with resolve conflict by *walking away.*

1	2	3	4	5	6	7
not much			some			a lot

5.   How much time do you spend with a parenting adult?

1	2	3	4	5	6	7
not much			some			a lot

6.   In my life, conflict has, on occasion, turned to violence.

1	2	3	4	5	6	7
never			sometimes			often

7.   I have witnessed a violent incident which started as a conflict.

1	2	3	4	5	6	7
never			sometimes			often

8.   I watch TV shows with violent content.

1	2	3	4	5	6	7
never			sometimes			often

Source: Lane-Garon, 1998.

Exhibit 5. Problem-Solving Strategies Survey, Form A

Prompts Generated by K–8 Students

Directions: Think about the following problem and pick the best solution.

1. A classmate spreads an untrue rumor about you and a girl.
    You would solve this problem by:
    A. Asking for mediation
    B. Talking to an adult
    C. Talking to the classmate who spread the rumor
    D. Other _____

2. A classmate threatens to beat you up if you don't give him your money.
    You would solve this problem by:
    A. Asking for mediation
    B. Talking to an adult
    C. Talking to the classmate with whom you've had the problem
    D. Other _____

Source: Lane-Garon, 1999.

Exhibit 6. Problem-Solving Strategies Survey, Form B

Prompts Generated by K–8 Students

_____   _____
          Name   Community role

Directions: Think about the following problem and pick the best solution.

1. You accidentally spread gossip about another student. This student is now mad.
    You would solve this problem by:
    A. Asking for mediation
    B. Talking to an adult
    C. Talking to the classmate with whom you've had the problem
    D. Other _____

2. You tease a certain student a lot and you've gotten in trouble for this in the past.
    You would solve this problem by:
    A. Asking for mediation
    B. Talking to an adult
    C. Talking to the classmate with whom you've had the problem
    D. Other _____

Source: Lane-Garon, 1999.

Pamela S. Lane-Garon is an associate professor of educational psychology at the Kremen School of Education and Human Development, California State University-Fresno. She is a mediator, a peer mediation trainer, and a researcher whose focus is social-cognitive change in youth as a result of mediation training and experience.

Tim Richardson has been principal of Herndon-Barstow Elementary for ten years. Partnering with Pamela Lane-Garon, the school earned the California School Boards Association Golden Bell Award in 2002 for its Peer Mediation project. Although it is the district's overflow school, with high rates of poverty and transience, its academic performance index has risen 131 points since beginning California's Immediate Intervention School Process (IIUSP) four years ago. It was awarded a fourth year of funding as a result of its success with these programs.

CONFLICTALK: An Instrument for Measuring Youth and Adolescent Conflict Management Message Styles

WILLIAM D. KIMSEY

REX M. FULLER

An instrument for assessing youth and adolescent conflict management message styles is presented. The CONFLICTALK instrument is intended as a tool for training in school-based peer mediator–conflict manager programs. Data collected from elementary, middle, and high school grades indicate that the scales used in CONFLICTALK measure typical responses to interpersonal and group conflict. Construct validity, using factor analysis, suggests that CONFLICTALK discriminates three conflict styles: (1) adversarial, (2) collaborative, and (3) avoidance across elementary and middle school levels. Conflict message wording for high school students appears less reliable.

Twelve-year-old John is excited to be included in his school's conflict management program but confused by the realization that others selected for the program don't agree with his understandings about conflict. In their training, John and his peers are given a variety of conflict situations for role playing and discussion. It comes as no small surprise to John that his classmates maintain significantly different perspectives concerning the conflict situations, and they advocate significantly different approaches to managing conflict.

Nor does it come as a surprise to practicing mediators and mediation trainers that people employ a variety of conflict management styles. In fact, interest in identifying and measuring conflict styles at the adult level appears to have begun in earnest in the 1960s (Blake and Mouton, 1964,

1968, 1969). In addition to language acquired through conflict resolution education (CRE) that connects course content with personal experiences of students taught at the elementary, middle, and high school levels (Jones and Compton, 2003), adolescent youth also assimilate a language that is unique to their culture and to their communication of conflict (Sandy, 2001). Sandy argues that if youth can use their language to express emotions in conflict (conflict styles), the adolescent is more skilled at management of conflict involving choices about self, other, and problems inherent in conflict resolution. Adolescent language is part of the adolescent culture, and it is the most sincere vehicle for communication; during the adolescent years, generally speaking, adult language is often perceived by adolescent youth as disingenuous; it is an authoritative turn-off. Since to date there are no conflict management message style surveys developed at the youth and adolescent levels, CONFLICTALK has been created to meet the practitioner's need where the adult surveys are not effective because of the language barrier.

Following the early work of Blake and Mouton (1970), the study of conflict management and mediation training has witnessed the development of many conflict style analysis instruments (Conrad, 1991; Goldstein, 1999; Louis, 1977; Rogers, 1987). In any mediation setting, identifying disputants' conflict styles plays an important role in the process of empowering the parties to reach a successful resolution to their dispute. Most conflict style instruments measure the conflict styles of adults; few, if any, have focused on the conflict styles demonstrated by children and adolescents. With the development of elementary, middle, and high school conflict manager mediation programs, the value of instruments such as CONFLICTALK, developed specifically for this audience, seems apparent. These tools are of great value because understanding one's own conflict style and the conflict styles employed by others increases our ability to successfully cope with and negotiate conflict situations.

Methodology

CONFLICTALK evolved through several iterations: an eighteen-item test was administered to samples; factors were analyzed; conflict management messages were edited; tests were readministered; and the process was repeated. Subject responses were analyzed using factor analysis. Following analysis and evaluation, individual items were edited and refocused.

Scale

The authors developed CONFLICTALK, an eighteen-item conflict style survey instrument, specifically for use in training elementary, middle, and high school conflict managers participating with in-school mediation or conflict management programs. The Ross-DeWine Conflict Management Message Style (CMMS) instrument (Ross and DeWine, 1988) was used as the prototype for the CONFLICTALK instrument; it was built on the premise that conflict management style can be identified via disputant message-producing behaviors. Ross and DeWine reference "the uncertainty of the existence of five styles" (p. 390) as identified by Blake and Mouton (1970) and Thomas and Kilmann (1974). CMMS identifies three message types: self-oriented, issue-oriented, and other-oriented. CONFLICTALK is, likewise, a self-report, untimed instrument designed to address conflict styles through messages used by elementary, middle, and high school–aged disputants in interpersonal conflict. In analyzing all eighteen items from the Ross-DeWine CMMS, we found a basis for conversion from adult wording in CMMS to youth-adolescent wording in CONFLICTALK; all eighteen items were subsequently converted. Consistent with CMMS, CONFLICTALK also identifies three conflict styles: self-focus (rhino), problem-focus (dolphin), and other-focus (ostrich). Animal symbols are used as mnemonic devices for the purpose of associating the stereotypically assigned animal behaviors consistent with the related conflict style(s).

CONFLICTALK presents subjects with eighteen phrases that might be expressed in a conflict situation. Subjects are asked to rate each phrase on a scale of 1 to 5 indicating that they "never say things like this" on one end of the continuum or "almost always say things like this" at the other end. These ratings are then calculated and scored to indicate the subject's conflict management style preferences in three conflict style categories: problem-focus (dolphin), self-focus (rhino), and other-focus (ostrich). Items three, five, seven, eleven, twelve, and seventeen are dolphin items. Items two, four, six, thirteen, fourteen, and fifteen are ostrich items. Items one, eight, nine, ten, sixteen, and eighteen are rhino items. Each statement is rated on a 5-point Likert-type scale. In this study, the problem-focus (dolphin) was operationally defined as showing concern for the cause of the conflict, being interested in finding the best solution, and acting cooperatively. The self-focus (rhino) was operationally defined as being self-centered, wanting one's own way, and acting aggressively. The other-focus (ostrich) was operationally defined as thinking conflict is bad, wanting the other to be happy, and acting passively.

Sample

In its present form, a random sample of 500 elementary, middle, and high school students were selected to participate in the study. The students ranged in grade from fourth to twelfth. The fourth- and fifth-grade sample was drawn from three elementary schools. The sixth- through eighth-grade subjects were from one middle school, and the ninth- through twelfth-grade surveys were collected from one high school. It is important to understand that all surveyed students had not received prior systematic training in conflict resolution or mediation as a part of this study. It is possible that individual students may have, at some time in their education, received conflict manager training, but it was not a consideration for this study's survey. Gender compositions for test samples were (1) elementary school, male = 127, female = 95; (2) middle school, male = 69, female = 64; and (3) high school, male = 80, female = 65. Race and ethnicity were not considered for this study.

Each subject was asked to complete the CONFLICTALK survey voluntarily and remain anonymous in order to respect confidentiality and obtain accurate results. Each subject volunteer was given a one-page CONFLICTALK survey with instructions explaining that the survey contained language that people sometimes use in an argument. Further, the instructions asked the subjects to think about each item and evaluate it to determine if it was something that they might say in a conflict situation. Participants were asked to rate each item on a scale of one to five, with no answers being necessarily right or wrong. At the bottom of the survey, there were two demographic items, one regarding subject sex and the other identifying the subject's grade level.

Results and Discussion

Factor analyses with Varimax rotation were conducted on three samples. Factor analysis identifies underlying constructs and is a typical test for construct validity. Samples for this study were selected from (1) elementary school grades four and five ($n = 222$); (2) middle school grades six, seven, and eight ($n = 133$); and (3) high school grades nine, ten, eleven, and twelve ($n = 145$). The following are factor structures for each of the groups. Factor loadings were expected to be at least .5 or better, with less than .4 on other factors. However, in four instances, loadings failed to meet the .5 but were evaluated as significant; eigenvalue equaled 1.0.

Table 1 reports the results of the factor analysis with Varimax rotation, in three sections; the first is for elementary school grades four and five.

Table 1. Factor Analysis with Varimax Rotation

Item	Factor 1	Factor 2	Factor 3
For Elementary School Grades Four and Five			
1. Can't you see how stupid you are?	−.02	**.64**	.04
2. I'm no good at this. I just don't know how to make you feel better.	.25	.09	**.43**
3. What's going on? We need to talk.	**.65**	−.08	.19
4. I'm no help to you, I never know what to say.	.16	.11	**.34**
5. We need to fix this.	**.71**	−.04	.18
6. I wish we could just avoid the whole thing.	.29	−.12	**.51**
7. Let's talk about this and find an answer.	**.71**	−.24	.02
8. Shut up! You're wrong! I'm not going to listen.	−.33	**.74**	.01
9. It's your fault! And, I'm never going to help you.	−.13	**.78**	.05
10. You will do as I say; I'm going to make you!	.01	**.79**	−.07
11. It will work if we work together.	**.78**	−.21	.15
12. We will work this thing out.	**.87**	−.13	.09
13. Okay, I give up, whatever you want.	.00	.04	**.60**
14. I don't want to do this anymore, let's quit and leave it alone.	−.12	.12	**.63**
15. This isn't going anywhere, let's just forget the whole thing, okay?	.09	.00	**.65**
16. If you won't do it, forget you; I'll just ask someone else.	−.16	**.66**	.27
17. We need to figure out what the problem is together.	**.80**	−.10	−.01
18. You can't do anything. Get out of my way and let me do it.	−.20	**.69**	.10
Percentage of variance	27.3	15.7	7.9
Total variance = 50.9%			
For Middle School Grades Six, Seven, and Eight			
1. Can't you see how stupid you are?	−.33	**.44**	.07
2. I'm no good at this. I just don't know how to make you feel better.	−.02	.19	**.48**
3. What's going on? We need to talk.	**.60**	−.29	.21
4. I'm no help to you, I never know what to say.	.09	.22	**.60**
5. We need to fix this.	**.76**	−.17	.03
6. I wish we could just avoid the whole thing.	.42	−.10	**.55**
7. Let's talk about this and find an answer.	**.82**	−.10	.08
8. Shut up! You're wrong! I'm not going to listen.	−.25	**.75**	.00
9. It's your fault! And, I'm never going to help you.	−.16	**.87**	.04
10. You will do as I say; I'm going to make you!	−.10	**.80**	−.02
11. It will work if we work together.	**.66**	−.25	−.01
12. We will work this thing out.	**.78**	−.21	.06

(Continued)

Table 1. Factor Analysis with Varimax Rotation (Continued)

For Middle School Grades Six, Seven, and Eight			
Item	*Factor 1*	*Factor 2*	*Factor 3*
13. Okay, I give up, whatever you want.	.05	.02	**.69**
14. I don't want to do this anymore, let's quit and leave it alone.	.04	.08	**.73**
15. This isn't going anywhere, let's just forget the whole thing, okay?	.00	−.23	**.62**
16. If you won't do it, forget you; I'll just ask someone else.	−.18	**.54**	.38
17. We need to figure out what the problem is together.	**.78**	−.04	.00
18. You can't do anything. Get out of my way and let me do it.	−.19	**.75**	.12
Percentage of variance	29.0	16.2	8.8
Total variance = 54.0%			
For High School Grades Nine, Ten, Eleven, and Twelve			
1. Can't you see how stupid you are?	.14	.03	.21
2. I'm no good at this. I just don't know how to make you feel better.	.34	.32	−.02
3. What's going on? We need to talk.	**.69**	.11	−.17
4. I'm no help to you, I never know what to say.	.03	**.56**	.14
5. We need to fix this.	**.76**	.09	−.12
6. I wish we could just avoid the whole thing.	.37	**.54**	−.04
7. Let's talk about this and find an answer.	**.77**	−.03	−.01
8. Shut up! You're wrong! I'm not going to listen.	−.09	.00	**.75**
9. It's your fault! And, I'm never going to help you.	−.04	.16	**.75**
10. You will do as I say; I'm going to make you!	−.04	−.01	**.73**
11. It will work if we work together.	**.78**	.02	.20
12. We will work this thing out.	**.83**	.00	.00
13. Okay, I give up, whatever you want.	.01	**.75**	.06
14. I don't want to do this anymore, let's quit and leave it alone.	−.08	**.75**	.13
15. This isn't going anywhere, let's just forget the whole thing, okay?	.18	**.72**	.06
16. If you won't do it, forget you; I'll just ask someone else.	.00	.40	.43
17. We need to figure out what the problem is together.	**.71**	.11	.00
18. You can't do anything. Get out of my way and let me do it.	−.12	.33	**.69**
Percentage of variance	22.0	18.3	9.0
Total variance = 50.0%			

Three factors emerged from the elementary school data (grades four and five). Factor 1 included the six conflict messages for measuring problem orientation with an emphasis on both goal and relationship. Conflict messages three, five, seven, eleven, twelve, and seventeen loaded significantly on factor 1, labeled "dolphin," a win-win, problem orientation (alpha reliability = .87).

Factor 2 emerged with six conflict messages for measuring self-orientation, with a high concern for personal goal achievement and a low concern for relationship. Conflict messages one, eight, nine, ten, sixteen, and eighteen met the criteria for item inclusion on factor 2, labeled "rhino," a win-lose, adversarial orientation (alpha reliability = .81).

Factor 3 identified six conflict messages associated with other orientation, with a low concern for both relationship and personal goal. Conflict messages two, four, six, thirteen, fourteen, and fifteen, albeit a little weak for messages two and four, accounted for the variance in factor 3, labeled "ostrich," a yield-lose, avoidance orientation (alpha reliability = .65).

These results are consistent with the hypothesized dimensions identified in the instrument CONFLICTALK. Construct validity for students in grades four and five appears stable with just over 50 percent of the variance accounted.

Table 1 also reports, in its second section, the results of the factor analysis with Varimax rotation for the middle school grades six, seven, and eight.

Three factors emerged from the middle school data. Factor 1 included the six conflict messages for measuring problem orientation, with an emphasis on both goal and relationship. Conflict messages three, five, seven, eleven, twelve, and seventeen loaded significantly on factor 1, labeled "dolphin," a win-win, problem orientation (alpha reliability = .87).

Factor 2 emerged with six conflict messages for measuring self-orientation, with a high concern for personal goal achievement and a low concern for relationship. Conflict messages one, eight, nine, ten, sixteen, and eighteen met the criteria for item inclusion on factor 2, labeled "rhino," a win-lose, adversarial orientation (alpha reliability = .81).

Factor 3 identified six conflict messages associated with other orientation, with a low concern for both relationship and personal goal. Conflict messages two, four, six, thirteen, fourteen, and fifteen, albeit a little weak for messages two and four, accounted for the variance in factor 3, labeled "ostrich," a yield-lose, avoidance orientation (alpha reliability = .65).

These results are consistent with the hypothesized dimensions identified in the instrument CONFLICTALK. Construct validity for students in grades six, seven, and eight appears stable with just under 55 percent of the variance accounted. These results are consistent with the elementary school analyses.

Table 1, the third section, reports the results of the factor analysis with Varimax rotation for the high school grades nine, ten, eleven, and twelve.

Factor analysis of the eighteen conflict messages for the high school data found a three-factor solution similar to the elementary and middle school data, yet some deviations from the hypothesized model for CONFLICTALK appear in the high school data. Factor 1 included the six conflict messages for measuring problem orientation with an emphasis on both goal and relationship (alpha reliability = .87). These results are consistent with the factor 1 findings for both elementary and middle school subjects. Factor 2 for high school students, however, identified the ostrich conflict style with conflict messages four, six, thirteen, fourteen, and fifteen as indicators of the avoidance, yield-lose orientation. However, conflict message two did not associate with the ostrich factor (alpha reliability = .63). Factor 3 also loaded differently with conflict messages eight, nine, ten, sixteen, and eighteen, meeting criteria for item selection with conflict message one being rejected (alpha reliability = .81). The total variance accounted for by the factor analysis of grades nine, ten, eleven, and twelve respondents was 50 percent. Construct validity for high school–aged subjects appears less stable for rhino and ostrich categories but stable for dolphin.

Conclusion

For grades four through eight the instrument appears to be valid and reliable. Data for grades nine through twelve suggest that CONFLICTALK has potential value, yet the factor loadings are not fully consistent with the elementary and middle school grades. The data and its consistency for grades four through eight are reinforced by the fact that when the instrument is completed by students in grades nine through twelve, construct validity for the instrument appears to diminish, suggesting that as subjects mature there is an evolution in their conflict message styles. Whereas the adult level instrument presented by Ross and DeWine is a valid instrument for measuring conflict styles for adults, the CONFLICTALK instrument appears to be a valid instrument for assessing elementary and middle school–age subjects. There is a clear need for the development of an instrument specifically designed for subjects in grades nine to twelve, who are characterized as an age group in transition from childhood to adulthood.

In short, CONFLICTALK is a reliable means to identify and describe conflict management styles demonstrated by elementary and middle school–aged students. School-based mediation programs are encouraged to use this instrument as a tool for training conflict managers/peer mediators as well as supplementing classroom instruction. If students during the elementary and middle school years gain a greater understanding of conflict styles and conflict management, perhaps, as they approach their high school years and beyond, their understanding of conflict will be more mature than that of students who do not receive instruction and training in conflict and mediation studies. CONFLICTALK can be helpful in achieving learning objectives related to skill competencies in the analysis and resolution of interpersonal conflict.

References

Blake, R., and Mouton, J. *The Managerial Grid.* Houston: Gulf, 1964.

Blake, R., and Mouton, J. *Corporate Excellence Through Grid Organization Development: A Systems Approach.* Houston: Gulf, 1968.

Blake, R., and Mouton, J. *Building a Dynamic Corporation Through Grid Organization Development.* Reading, Mass.: Addison-Wesley, 1969.

Blake, R., and Mouton, J. "The Fifth Achievement." In F. E. Janot (ed.), *Conflict Resolution Through Communication.* New York: HarperCollins, 1970.

Conrad, C. "Communication in Conflict: Style-Strategy Relationships." *Communication Monographs,* 1991, *58,* 135–153.

Goldstein, S. B. "Construction and Validation of a Conflict Communication Scale." *Journal of Applied Psychology,* 1999, *29* (9), 1803–1832.

Jones, T. S., and Compton, R. (eds.). *Kids Working It Out: Stories and Strategies for Making Peace in Our Schools.* San Francisco: Jossey-Bass, 2003.

Louis, M. R. "How Individuals Conceptualize Conflict: Identification of Steps in the Process and the Role of Personal/Development Factors." *Human Relations,* 1977, *30,* 451–467.

Rogers, S. J. "The Dynamics of Conflict Behavior in a Mediated Dispute." *Mediation Quarterly,* 1987, *18,* 61–71.

Ross, R. G., and DeWine, S. "Assessing the Ross-DeWine Conflict Management Message Style (CMMS)." *Management Communication Quarterly,* 1988, *1* (3), 389–413.

Sandy, S. V. "Conflict Resolution Education in the Schools: Getting There." *Conflict Resolution Quarterly,* 2001, *19* (2), 237–250.

Thomas, K., and Kilmann, R. *Thomas-Kilmann Conflict Mode Instrument.* Escondido, Calif.: Blanchard Training and Development, 1974.

William D. Kimsey is a professor of communication in the School of Communication Studies at James Madison University. He teaches courses in mediation and conflict studies, communication theory, and research methods. He serves as a consultant in communication and conflict resolution to business, government, and education.

Rex M. Fuller is a professor of communication studies in the School of Communication Studies at James Madison University. He teaches courses in the Mediation and Conflict Studies program and serves as a board member of the Community Mediation Center in Harrisonburg, Virginia.

Our Neighborhood: Using Entertaining Children's Television to Promote Interethnic Understanding in Macedonia

LISA SHOCHAT

Nashe Maalo *(Our Neighborhood in Macedonian) is a television series designed to encourage mutual respect and understanding among ethnic Albanian, Macedonian, Roma, and Turkish youths ages seven to twelve. Grounded in the belief that entertaining media programming can play an important role in conflict transformation,* Nashe Maalo's *research results show that the series is popular, that children understand what they watch, and that the series holds significant potential to affect children's attitudes and behavior.*

Media play a powerful role in shaping public consciousness throughout the world. In 1999, the Census Bureau reported that 98 percent of U.S. households have television sets (approximately 2.3 televisions per household).[1] Fifty-three percent of children age two through eighteen have a television in their bedroom (*Kids & Media at the New Millenium*, 1999). Although television is pervasive, research has shown that television content can serve as a negative influence on viewers' perceptions and behaviors. A recent review of research on the influences of media violence on social behavior states, "Research from some countries shows that, besides some desirable influences, media violence contributes to undesirable fear, erroneous conceptions of real violence, habituation to violence in the media,

NOTE: Nashe Maalo *has been financially supported by the British Department for International Development, the John D. and Catherine T. MacArthur Foundation, the Ministry of Foreign Affairs of The Netherlands, the Charles Stewart Mott Foundation, the Swedish International Development Agency, the Swiss Agency of Development and Cooperation, the United Nations Educational, Scientific, and Cultural Organization (UNESCO), the U.S. Agency for International Development, and the U.S. Institute of Peace.*

imitation, and, to some extent, destructive aggression—if other and far more decisive factors promoting destructive aggressiveness are also present" (von Feilitzen and Bucht, 2001, p. 48). In addition, negative images of different ethnic groups can serve to reinforce stereotypes: "The absence of [some ethnic groups portrayed in the media] suggests that they are not worthy of viewers' attention, while stereotyped or negatively-valued roles indicate that they are not worthy of respect" (Children Now, 1998, p. 1).

Despite the dire picture drawn by these examples, the power of the media can also be directed toward positive social change. Media and peace-building organizations around the world are developing new and experimental media initiatives that aim to complement conflict-resolution activities with popular entertainment and news media programming. In a recent publication on peace-building media, Ross Howard describes how the media can support the goals of conflict resolution: "It [media] functions as a channel of communication that counteracts misperceptions. It frames and analyzes the conflict, identifies the interests, defuses mistrust, provides safe emotional outlets, and more" (Howard, 2002, p. 4).

Search for Common Ground (SFCG) has implemented a variety of peace-building media projects in its twenty-year history.[2] These activities include facilitating dialogue on television, radio, and the Internet; establishing balanced sources for news and information in Burundi, Liberia, and Sierra Leone; highlighting areas of hope through radio and television documentaries in Angola; and modeling mutual respect and understanding through radio and television drama in Sub-Saharan Africa, South Eastern Europe, and Indonesia. This article uses the children's television series in Macedonia called *Nashe Maalo* as an example of how these media projects are developed and implemented and what can be deduced from impact research conducted thus far in the project's history.

Interethnic Relations in Macedonia

Recent conflicts such as the war in Macedonia in 2001 and the Kosovo crisis of 1999 dealt a hard blow to Macedonia's economy and its internal interethnic relations. In this nation of two million people, the majority Macedonians (roughly 65 percent) live alongside ethnic Albanians (roughly 25 percent)[3] and small percentages of Turks, Roma, Serbs, and Vlachs, in a complex maze of ethnic, cultural, and religious differences. It is one of the most ethnically mixed countries in the region, yet its society is profoundly segregated.

The media and education systems play a major role in encouraging these divisions. Television and radio stations operate exclusively in the Albanian or Macedonian languages and present the viewpoint of their respective ethnic groups. The public school system is highly segregated. Children of a single ethnicity grow up learning together and speaking one language in the classroom. Friendships are therefore formed almost exclusively within ethnic groups and rarely cross linguistic and cultural lines. As a result, the people of Macedonia have few windows into the concerns and experiences of other ethnic groups. The lack of interethnic contact gives rise to prejudice and fear, sowing the seeds of instability and, potentially, of deadly conflict. *Nashe Maalo* is a central element of SFCG's systematic approach to building tolerance and understanding across these barriers in Macedonia.

Working with Children and Media: Building from SFCG's Strengths

Common Ground media projects are usually designed as components within a multifaceted strategy for peace building in a targeted society. In Macedonia, children and media professionals were identified by SFCG early on as key actors in building Macedonia's future. Beginning in 1994, Search for Common Ground began implementing projects that aimed to bridge some of the divisions among Macedonia's communities:

- Environmental stewardship clubs, where children of different backgrounds developed relationships with one another while working together to restore monuments and other public spaces

- Joint reporting projects, where reporters from the major Albanian-language and Macedonian-language newspapers worked together to coauthor weekly feature stories that were printed in both publications with shared bylines

- Conflict resolution games programs used by fourth-grade students in schools across Macedonia to learn communication and problem-solving skills

The opportunity for developing a children's television series would allow SFCG to build from its strengths in working with children and the media to create a medium that would have the potential to reach a large number of children and their parents with messages of intercultural understanding and role models for dealing with conflict in everyday life.

Production Methodology

Nashe Maalo aims to bridge the cultural divide by offering children a window into each other's lives and by modeling positive strategies for coping with conflict. The program's stories seek to help children appreciate their differences as well as the values they share. The program concept is based on a body of research indicating that television has a profound effect on children's perceptions (Cairns, 1989; Children Now, 1998; Graves, 2000). For example, a meta-analysis of more than thirty-nine studies of the impact of television on children concludes that "Children exposed to prosocial content [on television] have more positive social interactions, show more altruistic behavior and self-control, and have less stereotyped views of others" (Mares, 1996, p. 19). Young people are acutely aware of, and influenced by, the images presented on television and other media.

In order for an educational television program to be successful in achieving outcomes of this type, it must effectively blend clearly researched curricular goals with the elements that make a children's series successful: it grabs kids' imagination, is entertaining, and makes kids want to see more. For the *Nashe Maalo* project, this meant that a large team of people from different professional and cultural backgrounds would need to collaborate actively to maximize the potential of the series.

The first phase of this cooperative effort would be to define the project's goals in a series curriculum. A team composed of Macedonian conflict resolution professionals, child psychologists, researchers, creative writers, and producers convened in the fall of 1998 to develop the curriculum for the series. On the basis of an assessment of the learning needs and capabilities of Macedonian children between the ages of seven and twelve, the group identified three major categories of goals for the series: (1) promoting intercultural understanding, (2) offering strategies for conflict prevention in a multicultural context, and (3) teaching conflict resolution skills for dealing with conflict in everyday life. This series curriculum would serve as the backbone for the series and has guided researchers in designing studies to measure impact.

The Production Process

Every Common Ground television production aims to engage balanced participation, build local capacity, and model conflict resolution skills both behind the camera and on the television screen. When the *Nashe Maalo* producers were ready to begin designing the characters and storylines for the series, they recruited a team of four writers to create the stories. The team was intentionally assembled to reflect the cultural and gender diversity of the country, which was supplemented with the conflict resolution and cultural expertise of content advisors and cultural consultants. Since then, production apprenticeships have been established to broaden the representation behind the camera further to include more women and people from other ethnic backgrounds on the writing team as well as on the production crew.

The story of *Nashe Maalo* features a group of children of Albanian, Macedonian, Roma, and Turkish ethnicities who live in the neighborhood of a magical apartment building. These kids share a secret that binds them together: the building is alive! Her name is Karmen and, in addition to being the kids' confidante and friend, she possesses the power to magically transport them into their neighbors' cultural and psychological milieus. These scenes open the eyes of the characters to other people's ways of thinking and living.

Each episode of *Nashe Maalo* is designed to be entertaining and convey designated elements of the curricular goals. Creative producers and writing coaches from Great Britain and the United States worked with the writers to make the stories and dialogue as exciting as possible. Meanwhile, a team of conflict resolution experts and cultural consultants reviewed the scripts for their educational content. The process stretched the capacities of both teams and challenged them to be patient and understanding with one another throughout the process.

The production phase is the most resource-heavy period of each year-long season. It is the process that transforms the scripts into dramatic television episodes. The crew of more than one hundred people must work together on a tight schedule for rehearsing, preparing, and shooting each episode. Postproduction (editing, animation, music, and subtitling) begins as soon as the first day's material has been shot. Preparation is essential.

The program is produced in the Macedonian language, with roughly 20 percent of the dialogue in the Albanian, Romany, and Turkish languages. The series is broadcast on A1 TV (an independent Macedonian-language broadcaster) with subtitles of all non-Macedonian-language material. Albanian-language stations air a version with Albanian subtitles for all the dialogue not in Albanian.

Finally, outreach projects are designed to deepen the impact of the television series. Thus far, outreach projects have included parent-teacher guides, a pop music video and CD, a children's magazine, and an interactive website (www.nashemaalo.com).

Building Local Production Capacity

The opening of the first season of *Nashe Maalo* was broadcast nationally in Macedonia in October 1999. As of the fall of 2002, four seasons (thirty-four episodes) have been produced and broadcast in Macedonia, and scriptwriters are currently developing storylines for season five. Each year, there has been a focus on building the capacity of local writers, cultural consultants, researchers, and producers to manage the project from beginning to end. Particularly with the writing process, there has been a significant shift of control of the stories' content from international television advisors to the local team. In addition, production responsibilities have also been transferred from international experts to a Macedonian-Albanian team of producers who work together to manage the production crew, schedule, and budget for transforming the scripts into finished dramatic episodes.

The Role of Research in *Nashe Maalo*

Research occurs at every stage of development in a curriculum-based television series like *Nashe Maalo*. Especially in cases of programs that target children, the entertainment value must be high to ensure the prolonged, repeat viewing that is needed for learning. Therefore research seeks to measure a progression of impact with the target audience, ranging from measuring people's access to the program, viewership rates, and comprehension of the content to attitude and behavior change as a result of watching. Studies have occurred intermittently over the course of the project and have attempted to delve deeper into questions of impact as the project has developed. To suggest this continuum of impact visually:

Reach/appeal → comprehension → attitude change → behavior change

Measuring Reach

Selecting appropriate media, determining the best times and strategies for delivery, and promoting broadcast are all activities that support and encourage access to the programming. Once broadcast has been launched, viewership studies take place. To determine viewership levels of the series among Macedonian children and their parents, Search for Common Ground, in collaboration with Klime Babunski, of the NGO Pro Media and in association with Eve Hall, research director for the project, conducted in 2000 a nationally representative survey of twelve hundred children and their parents. The sample was stratified, and representative of the ethnic and geographic distribution of people across the country. The twelve hundred interviews included an even distribution of children who had just completed grades two through eight (ages eight to fourteen) and one of their parents. Interviews were conducted by a field researcher, who visited the families in their homes and interviewed each parent and child individually. The purpose of this survey, conducted in May 2000, was to ascertain awareness and popularity of *Nashe Maalo,* as well as key factors contributing to the public's reaction.

Perhaps the most convincing evidence of the success of *Nashe Maalo* is its popularity among children of all ethnic groups. According to the results of the viewership survey, more than 75 percent of children in Macedonia report watching the program, and the overwhelming majority rate it as good or excellent. This is significant because children can learn only from programming they are willing to watch. In addition, about half of the parents had watched the program and discussed it with their children. Considering the controversial nature of *Nashe Maalo* and its educational content, it is noteworthy that children and their parents find the series and its characters appealing. Also worth noting is that Macedonian and Albanian children are equally likely to have heard of *Nashe Maalo* and are just as likely to watch it.

Formative Research

Formative research feeds into the stories and characters, making them relevant, understandable, and appealing to members of the target audience. Studies of this kind often use qualitative methods such as interviews and focus groups to get a rich understanding of how children are responding to the materials. For *Nashe Maalo,* qualitative interviews with young viewers occur after production has been completed on each new season of episodes.

The research conducted on episodes from season two was designed specifically to inform the writers and producers before writing started on season three. These studies were conducted by Mirjana Najchevska, senior researcher at the Institute for Sociological, Political, and Juridical Research at the University of Skopje, in association with Eve Hall. One-hundred and sixty ten- and eleven-year-olds from Albanian, Macedonian, Roma, and Turkish ethnicities were interviewed after viewing four episodes from season two. The objective of the study was to test such vital information as understanding of the overall storyline, central conflict and ethnic dimensions, appreciation of the use of different languages, and appeal and identification with characters across cultural lines. In addition, a segment of the study was devoted to children's lives, interests, and concerns—information that will be used to form content in the episodes that reflects the real lives of children in Macedonia today.

The results of the study were presented at a conference in December 2000 to the writing, research, and production teams. Interestingly, there was no significant difference of attitudes or comprehension across ethnic lines, although there was some variation according to what city the respondents were from. The results included these noteworthy points:

• Appeal: The research informed us that children enjoy the series very much. Children appreciate the episodes because "there are children like us in it." They particularly like the animated character of Karmen, the games, the friendship of the children, the fun, the humor, and the music.

• Comprehension and credibility: In general, the children are able to retell the entire literal content of every episode, they understand the main conflict, and they understand the global message of each episode. Also very relevant to creating episodes in the third season, the children find the *Nashe Maalo* world to be believable.

• Problem solving: The show's central character, Karmen (who has no specific ethnic affiliation and who serves as a primary conveyor of mutual-respect messages), was popular among children of all ethnic groups. This is an indicator that the program's core messages are finding a receptive audience. Nevertheless, the children often thought that it was Karmen who solved the problem and not the child characters themselves. Therefore, it was decided that Karmen would more clearly be defined as a wise friend to the children, but that the young characters themselves would more overtly model their personal agency in problem solving in future episodes of the show.

• Ethnic diversity: Children often had a hard time telling what ethnic group the characters were from, yet they expressed enjoyment of the differing ethnicities when they were highlighted. The research shows that, faced with characters of different backgrounds, kids tend to identify with what the characters have in common—that they are good at sports, are funny, or are good dancers. Since one goal of the series is to promote tolerance of differences, the team decided that, in the third season, they would draw differences more clearly and strive to convey the message that differences are positive.

Bearing in mind the results from the research just described, writers went to work in creating a new season of episodes for 2001. After season three's episodes were completed, a comparable study was conducted so that the *Nashe Maalo* team could gauge their progress in addressing the issues raised in the previous year. In October 2001, 310 children between the ages of ten and eleven from four regions of Macedonia participated in the study. Equal numbers of children from Albanian, Macedonian, Roma, and Turkish backgrounds watched four new episodes and then were interviewed in ethnically and gender-homogeneous groups of five children. In total, eighty children watched each episode. As in the study from season two, the objective was to test children's appeal and comprehension of the episodes. Results show some improvements since season two in making the *Nashe Maalo* world more understandable. Most children managed to connect Karmen with the resolution of conflict. They expressed enjoyment and appreciation for how Karmen allows the child characters themselves to realize a problem and to find the most beneficial solution. In addition, the researchers found that children had no difficulty in identifying the ethnicity of the characters and continued to express appreciation for those episodes that explored ethnic difference.

Qualitative studies such as these can also explore the educational capacity of the television program. Najchevska states, "The educational nature of *Nashe Maalo* is a major feature in the reviews of participating children; they have independently determined that there are ideas and lessons to be learned from *Nashe Maalo,* and that they have themselves learned a lot. Said some study participants: 'I learned that I should be the way I am'; 'Until now I thought that Macedonians and Albanians only fought, but I don't think so anymore'" (Najchevska, 2001, p. 5).

The continued appeal and comprehension expressed by children was particularly important given that a violent conflict between the Macedonian government and an ethnic Albanian militia group had taken place only six months prior to the study. The researchers stated, "In the context of an exclusively negative media campaign aimed at inciting enmity and hatred between members of different ethnic communities, this series appears as a beacon of light, around which the children's positive emotions and positive energy coalesce" (Najchevska, 2001, p. 4).

Measuring Impact

The studies described here can help project implementers understand whether the programming is popular, how many people view it and how often, and whether they understand the major themes presented in the program. The final category of research on curriculum-based programs is the most difficult to conduct, yet is the most important.

After the first season of the *Nashe Maalo* episodes was produced, a study was conducted to investigate the impact the series was having on children's attitudes. The research effort was led by Najchevska, in association with Charlotte Cole, vice president of education and research for Sesame Workshop, and Search for Common Ground. The study examined the children's perceptions of each other, their willingness to interact with members of each other's cultures, their awareness of each other's languages, and the appeal of the program.

Methodology

Ideally, impact studies are designed at the beginning of the project and include gathering baseline data before the broadcast has been launched. Researchers devise instruments that most effectively measure the indicators set out in the curriculum. In Macedonia, a one-on-one interview instrument was devised to test children's attitudes about members of ethnic and gender groups in Macedonian society. Once the instrument had been pretested, trained data collectors individually interviewed 240 children in their home languages at eight schools in the Skopje region (sixty ten-year-olds from each of four ethnic groups) prior to and after viewing the series' eight episodes. Within each group, a roughly equal number of boys and girls participated. Children viewed videotaped versions of the series over the course of several months and were interviewed again after exposure to all eight episodes. The study began in October 1999 (before the first broadcast of the TV series commenced). Data were subjected to analysis of variance models and other standard statistical techniques. Including a control group in this kind of study would further help to isolate causation, if time and budget allow.

Findings

There are several interesting insights from the research on the *Nashe Maalo* program.

Overcoming Stereotypes

Nashe Maalo was found to have a very positive impact on children's views of themselves and others. When asked to describe members of the Albanian, Macedonian, Roma, and Turkish ethnic groups prior to viewing, many children demonstrated negative, stereotyped perceptions. After viewing, many children offered more positive descriptions when presented with images of people from other ethnic groups or their own. Macedonian children showed the greatest positive changes in perceptions of other ethnic groups. This evolution of attitudes among the dominant ethnic group is one of the most powerful findings of our research. Albanian children showed the greatest positive changes in perceptions of their own ethnic group (Figure 1).

It is also worth noting that Turkish children's responses showed both a positive self-image as well as a consistently positive description of the Macedonian individuals. Although most Turkish children (85 percent) provided positive descriptions of the Turkish man, it is striking that both before and after viewing the majority (66 percent) also offered positive descriptions of the Macedonian.

Figure 1. Increase in Positive Descriptions of Individuals from Each Ethnic Group by All Children Interviewed

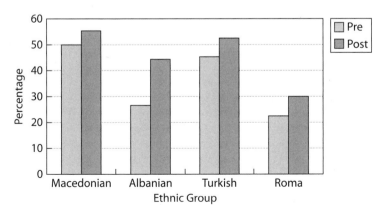

Recognizing Each Other's Languages

Not surprisingly, before viewing, nearly all of the children identified the Macedonian language, but fewer were able to identify the Albanian, Turkish, and Romany languages.

Furthermore, group analyses revealed important differences in the language awareness of children from different ethnic groups. Macedonian children, who are the least exposed to these other languages, were the least capable of identifying languages other than their own prior to viewing. Turkish children, however, were the best at other-language identification (97 percent of the Turkish children correctly identified all of the languages). It is an encouraging testament to the power of the program that, after viewing, recognition of minority languages improved across all ethnic lines, but most dramatically among Macedonian children.

Learning to Live Together

Prior to viewing, the majority (67 percent) of children indicated a reluctance to invite children from other ethnic groups into their homes. After viewing, there was an increase in the number of ethnic Macedonian children who expressed a willingness to invite others (Albanians, Roma, and Turks) into their homes (Figure 2).

The Roma children's responses are of special interest. Although only 40 percent provided positive descriptions of the picture representing their own ethnic group, the majority of Roma children offered positive descriptions of Macedonians. Such findings are suggestive of the potency of the dominant (Macedonian) culture and its impact on the Roma vision of

Figure 2. Change in Percentage of Ethnic Macedonian Children Willing to Invite a Child from Another Ethnic Group to Their Home

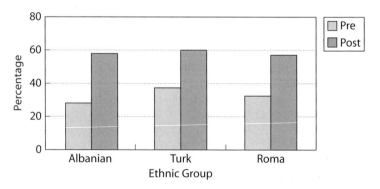

themselves. This assessment was shared by children from other groups, who judged the Roma less positively than they judged members of other ethnic groups. Projects such as *Nashe Maalo* hold the potential to affect this image of the Roma positively by depicting activities and occupations that counter ingrained, negative stereotypes.

Nashe Maalo writers and producers have responded to these findings by developing storylines and characters aimed at raising the image of Roma people among the Roma and non-Roma viewers alike. In some episodes, new role models have been presented, such as a Roma girl who is exceptionally good at math. In other episodes, a character realizes that she should not be embarrassed to have a Roma friend, and the adult characters show that no matter what cultural background, parents always worry about their children when they are late in arriving home.

Responding to Changes in the Conflict Context

As mentioned earlier, the social and political landscape has continued to shift since the first impact study was conducted in 2000. Particularly after the conflict in 2001, project staff were interested to know how children's perceptions had changed. Therefore, the research team, headed by Violeta Petrovska Beshka, repeated the baseline study that was initially conducted in 1999, in order to understand the impact the conflict had on children's lives. The results of this study had a strong immediate formative value in remapping the conflict, presenting valuable information on how new episodes could address the changing situation. As the program continues to evolve into future seasons, those data will be compared with follow-up studies to measure further changes.

Conclusion

Taken together, the findings from the studies point to the value of *Nashe Maalo* as a potent social intervention. In addition to providing an entertaining television program for youth, *Nashe Maalo* serves as a positive influence on its young viewers. As of spring 2003, *Nashe Maalo* has joined a number of efforts in Macedonia to promote multiculturalism. Since the launch of the *Nashe Maalo* theme song in 1999, more and more young pop musicians are recording multilingual songs; the national television network *MTV* is about to launch the first-ever multilingual television station. Perhaps most remarkably, DUI, the political party that emerged from the former Albanian insurgent National Liberation Army, has had ethnic Macedonians joining its ranks throughout 2002. When asked to explain why and how this could be happening, their verbatim answer was that they were using *"Nashe Maalo* logic." In this respect, *Nashe Maalo* has come to symbolize the possibility of true interethnic cooperation across the country.

Beyond Macedonia, *Nashe Maalo* is one of many new efforts to use the media creatively in countering stereotypes. Children's television programs as well as radio soap operas for youth are currently developed as part of multifaceted initiatives to promote mutual understanding. Some examples are *Gimme6,* a children's program developed to promote mutual understanding among children in Cyprus; *Rechov Sumsum/Shara'a Simsim,* a television series modeled after *Sesame Street* and designed to present messages of mutual respect and understanding to young Israeli and Palestinian children; and *What's the Story?,* an educational television comedy designed as a resource for the Curriculum for Mutual Understanding in Northern Ireland's schools. Each project is based on a curriculum; uses outreach projects to help deepen impact; and is the product of creative collaboration among educators, local experts on the conflict, and producers. The production methodology is based on more than three decades of experience in producing educational television for children, while the specific application to conflict resolution goals is still very new. The results of impact studies on these projects not only help to improve the individual projects but will also inform practitioners and donor partners who are interested in using television to promote peace-building efforts in other contexts. If there is hope for building mutual respect and understanding in conflict zones, it lies with the country's young citizens. Efforts such as *Nashe Maalo* are a positive step toward a better, more peaceful future.

Notes

1. U.S. Census Bureau, *Statistical Abstract of the United States: 2001.* (www.census.gov/)

2. Search for Common Ground (Washington, D.C.) and its partner organization, the European Centre for Common Ground (Brussels), are independent, nongovernmental organizations dedicated to transforming conflict into cooperative action. Common Ground Productions (based in Washington, D.C., and Brussels) provides support to all Common Ground radio and television initiatives internationally (www.sfcg.org).

3. Population statistics are from the 1994 census from the Republic of Macedonia (www.maknews.com/html/mia_census.html).

References

Cairns, E. "Social Identity and Intergroup Conflicts in Northern Ireland: A Development Perspective." In J. Harbinson (ed.), *Growing Up in Northern Ireland.* Belfast: Stranmills College, 1989.

Children Now. *A Different World: Children's Perceptions of Race and Class in the Media* (Report). Oakland, Calif.: Children Now, 1998.

Graves, S. B. "Television and Prejudice Reduction: When Does Television as a Vicarious Experience Make a Difference?" *Journal of Social Issues,* 2000, *55* (4), 707–725.

Howard, R. *An Operational Framework for Media and Peacebuilding.* Vancouver, B.C.: IMPACS (Institute for Media, Policy and Civil Society), 2002.

Kids & Media at the New Millennium: A Comprehensive National Analysis of Children's Media Use. Kaiser Family Foundation, Nov., 1999.

Mares, M. L. *Positive Effects of Television on Social Behavior: A Meta-Analysis* (No. 3). Philadelphia: Annenberg Public Policy Center, University of Pennsylvania, 1996.

Najchevska, M. *Episode Study on Nashe Maalo: Season Three.* Skopje: Institute for Sociological, Political, and Juridical Research, University of Skopje, 2001.

U.S. Census Bureau. *Statistical Abstract of the United States: 2001.* Washington, D.C.: Government Printing Office, 2001.

Von Feilitzen, C., and Bucht, C. "Reception and Influences of the Media." *Outlooks on Children and Media: Children and Media Violence Yearbook 2001.* Goteborg, Sweden: UNESCO International Clearinghouse of Children and Violence on the Screen (Nordicom), 2001.

Lisa Shochat currently manages development and research for Common Ground Productions, the media division of SFCG. Previously, she worked as a mediator-facilitator for the Center for Resolution of Environmental Disputes and administered mediation training through the Institute for Study of Alternative Dispute Resolution in California. She holds an M.A. in sociology from Humboldt State University and a B.A. from the University of California-Santa Cruz; her research has included programs in Macedonia, Hungary, Mexico, Burundi, and the United States.

Exploring the Intragroup Conflict Constructs and Behaviors of African American Public School Children in an Inner-City Conflict Resolution Education (CRE) Program

K. MICHELLE SCOTT

The Consortium on Negotiation and Conflict Resolution's (CNCR) Conflict Resolution in Schools Program (CRiSP) conducted a two-year study of inner-city African American public school children to discern any conflict constructs and behaviors that were apparent in the children's intragroup interactions. This article presents findings of the CNCR study, including three emergent themes—fears of victimization, identity conflict, and core values—that were consistently apparent in the children's demonstrations of intragroup conflict constructs and behaviors.

Conflict resolution researchers, theorists, and educators are becoming increasingly aware of the necessity for conflict resolution education (CRE) literature to address the needs and perspectives of discrete groups within our culturally diverse population. However, the Eurocentric values and attitudes that pervade traditional public education and training curricula (Banks, 1995) continue to permeate many mainstream CRE programs. Although "some of the [CRE] literature does discuss ways to make an essentially Eurocentric model more culturally approachable" (Baker, French, Trujillo, and Wing, 2000, p. 69), many conventional CRE programs tend to focus superficially on intergroup ("us-them") patterns of conflict (Bowland, 2000) rather than the intragroup values that may

NOTE: *This research was conducted while I was working as an intern with the Consortium on Negotiation and Conflict Resolution. I wish to thank the CNCR directors, the student-teachers, and the children for contributing to this project.*

provide the impetus for those intergroup interactions. Accordingly, Hairston (1999) argues that too little research on the conflict orientations of groups with nonmajority cultural experiences has led to a "culturally specific void" (p. 357) in the CR literature; thus, the knowledge and skills of CR practitioners as they relate to diverse perspectives are left wanting. The consequences of this void became apparent during the National Conference on Peacemaking and Conflict Resolution's (NCPCR) Cultural Bridges Coalition meeting when Native, African, Latin, and Asian American participants indicated that with regard to "cultural competence," mainstream conflict resolution processes mandated "vast adaptations" on their parts (Baker, French, Trujillo, and Wing, 2000). In other words, there was enough variation between the mainstream conflict resolution processes and those typically used by these participants that they felt the need to exert immense effort to adapt to the mainstream processes.

Indeed, states Baker, "there has been an abundance of information published on conflict resolution education in general and mediation in particular. [Yet], there is much less research done and even published on the effect of conflict resolution education on diverse populations, let alone from the perspective of those from diverse populations" (Baker, French, Trujillo, and Wing, 2000, p. 64). Hairston (1999) proposes that the absence of culturally specific research and literature produces a "hegemonic control of knowledge" and "renders issues of concern to African Americans unimportant and unworthy of scholarly attention" (p. 362).

From 1999 to 2001, the research-driven Consortium on Negotiation and Conflict Resolution (CNCR) initiated a series of case studies of inner-city African American public school children to discern any conflict constructs and behaviors that were apparent in the children's intragroup interactions. The consortium was motivated along this line of inquiry on the basis of (1) the perceived void in conflict resolution education literature with regard to targeting the values, needs, and interests of members of discrete, traditionally disenfranchised groups (Hairston, 1999; Baker, French, Trujillo, and Wing, 2000; and Bowland, 2000); (2) the implications of theories related to the influence of "transgenerationally transmitted trauma" on the intragroup conflict orientations of members of traditionally oppressed populations (Volkan, 1997; Scott, 2000); and (3) the growing interest in the institutionalization of CRE programs in American public school settings (Inger, 1991; Carruthers and others, 1996; Crawford and Bodine, 1996; Jones, Batton, and Carruthers, 2000).

CNCR is a cross-disciplinary, interinstitutional organization that studies the institutionalization of conflict prevention and resolution in complex organizations. Since 1995, much of CNCR's research and practice has been conducted in the education arena. The consortium is located within Georgia State University's College of Law and has received funding from the U.S. Department of Education to support the conduct of CRE research. A major component of CNCR from 1998 to 2001 was the Conflict Resolution in Schools Program (CRiSP), a clinical service-learning project that trained college students ("student-teachers") to teach conflict resolution theory and skills to children and personnel within public school systems designated by CNCR's directors and grantors.

This article presents the findings of the research initiatives undertaken on behalf of the consortium's CRiSP during a two-year period from 1999 to 2001 and shares the lessons learned about the intragroup conflict constructs and behaviors of those children of African descent enrolled in the CRiSP's CRE project. It should be noted that within the public school system used for this study, students were categorized on the basis of the racial designations "black," "white," "Hispanic," and "other." However, "even though race is a core feature of identity" (Gadlin, 1994, p. 36), to avoid the reductionism of identity politics that tends to occur when presumptions are made that sociological constructs such as race, class, or socioeconomics single-handedly account for differences in group behaviors (Gadlin, 1994), references to participants will be consistent with these designations: *African American* for participants of African descent, *European American* for participants of European descent, *Latino* for participants of Hispanic descent, and *Multiethnic* for participants of mixed descent. Thus, for our purposes the phrase *ethnic group* and the term *ethnicity* are used to suggest a prevalently shared cultural, social, political, and economic identity (Davis, 1996; Avrouch, 2000) that is also inclusive of race. Therefore, references to a *multiethnic* setting should be taken to indicate one in which the majority of the children are not presumed to have a prevalently shared cultural, social, political, economic, *and* racial identity.

Review of the Literature

Despite their prevalence, intragroup conflict orientations and their influence on intragroup and intergroup interactions have received too little attention from the discipline of CR.

The "Void" in CRE Literature

However, the limited discipline-specific literature is not a complete hindrance to the advancement of CRE initiatives since the interdisciplinary nature of conflict studies does allow the cross-referencing of literature from sociology, psychology, communication, education, and other programs of study. Fortunately for the purposes of this study, there are non-CR theorists whose research can indirectly influence CRE practice concerns with regard to African American children. For example, in Thomas's study (2000) of African American parenting techniques, she found that many African American parents were concerned about how their children's experiences with societal oppression, racism, and prejudice would lead to conflict behaviors associated with gangs and substance abuse. Concerns of this type were validated when psychologists conducting a study of adolescent African Americans found that "recognition of racism was significantly associated with increased problem behaviors and drug use, and that individuals who perceive society as being racist had less optimal psychologic and behavior profiles" (Resnicow and others, 1999). In fact, states Robinson, "a vast amount of research in the USA has shown that African American children may suffer from racial group identification difficulties due to the effects of discrimination and racism" (Robinson, 2000, p. 5).

In her consideration of violence among African American youth, Prothrow-Stith (1991) explored theories involving "free-floating anger" (Ramey, 1980), black self-hatred, poverty, gangs, drugs, and the high homicide rate among young black males. She concluded that "an epidemic of violence in the poorest of our poor neighborhoods is decimating a generation of men of color" (p. 64). In fact, the victimization of African American children occurs far too often at the hands of other African American children (Hanish, 2000). This suggests that although "interethnic conflict has been a recurring problem in the United States, particularly in schools" (Yager and Rotheram-Borus, 2000, p. 291), the intraethnic conflict orientations of African American youth may also be an area that mandates the attention of CR and CRE researchers.

Transgenerational Trauma and Intragroup Conflict

In addition to having conflict orientations that may be associated with their own lived experiences of racism, oppression, and violence, some African American adolescents may also be confronted with latent conflict as a consequence of transgenerationally transmitted traumas (Volkan, 1997; Apprey, 1998; Scott, 2000). This is because "the complexity of African American identity reflects centuries of a transgenerational haunting associated with the pain of colonialism, slavery, exploitation and discrimination . . . mental representations of the pain are endured through [intragroup] verbal and non-verbal transmissions" (Scott, 2000, p. 11). According to Volkan (1997), mental representations of a group's shared, massive trauma (for example, the massacre of Native Americans, the Jewish Holocaust, the enslavement of African Americans) are deposited into the psyches of subsequent generations and often manifested by those generations through internalized aggression. In other words, members of the group turn the angst associated with the group's experience of the trauma inward (see Apprey, 1998).

Certainly, the complexity of social behaviors and relations inherent in the African American community is too elaborate to be reduced to one theory (Scott, 2000), that is, transgenerated trauma. However, where transgenerated trauma is apparent, adolescents may have unwittingly internalized negative self-beliefs that influence their conflict constructs and behaviors within and apart from their communal group. For example, Hall (1995) points out that in the African American community "light skin is the point of reference for attractiveness and dark skin is necessarily threatening" (p. 176). Accordingly, he posits: "African Americans may develop a disdain for dark skin because the disdain is an expression of dominant culture ideals. It [dark skin] is regarded by the various institutions as an obstacle . . . and is associated with psychic conflict" (p. 173). Consequently, some researchers now associate racial and ethnic identity with psychological well-being (Resnicow and others, 1999) where self-esteem, along with dimensions of cultural pride and attitudes toward academic success (Robinson, 2000; Scott, 2000) are positively correlated to racial identity.

In his study of violence among at-risk middle school and high school students, Lockwood (1997) determined that a cultural value system that prefers violence as a form of retribution was "at the heart of" many conflicts among students. According to Lockwood, the children in his study demonstrated "a preference for violent retaliation over other forms of redress, a strong belief in punishment and a sensitivity to perceived injustice and mistreatment" (p. 10) as core values. Thus, Lockwood's study strongly suggests that shared cultural experiences are related to distinctive conflict orientations and values.

Efforts to create culturally informed CRE programs must give diligent consideration to how the lived experiences of discrete cultural groups influence members' conflict orientations, constructs, and behaviors. After all, the tendency to misdiagnose the symptoms of conflict is one of the leading inhibitors to successful CRE programs (see Jones, Batton, and Carruthers, 2000).

The Research Study

CNCR researchers were concerned about the degree to which intragroup patterns of conflict may or may not influence intergroup patterns of conflict, the extent to which intragroup patterns of conflict confirmed or disconfirmed theories of transgenerated trauma, and the extent to which CRE efforts should or should not be expected to address intragroup conflict constructs and behaviors as a basis for attending to intergroup conflict issues. Generally, it was felt that this study could be a starting point for the exploration of these more expansive concerns. The case study approach seemed most appropriate for our goals "to gain a better understanding of the complexities of human interactions" (Marshall and Rossman, 1995, p. 15) by focusing on one or more distinguishable cases (Denzin and Lincoln, 1998).

We focused on the conflict experiences and behaviors of inner-city African American adolescents enrolled in public school settings by extending the inquiry of each bounded system to a comparative study. The "comparative" nature of the study involved our comparisons of the African American children's conflict constructs and behaviors in the three settings where the CRiSP CRE initiative was conducted. These settings consisted of (1) an "in-school" program where participation was mandatory according to students' enrollment in a course where they earned credit and grades for their participation; (2) a community-based after-school program where middle school students were voluntary participants on the basis of their enrollment with the community center; and (3) an on-site after-school program where students were required to participate. In the second and third cases, the students did not receive grades for their participation. The sample of participants consisted of the African American adolescents enrolled in these inner-city settings.

To gather data, we used a primarily narrative structure that incorporated critical phenomenological (Schutz, 1970) and ethnomethodological

(Garfinkel, 1967) concepts for an inductive analysis. Data were primarily procured through focus groups where the adolescents were asked questions related to their definitions of conflict, their responses to conflict, their school's responses to conflict, and their observations of conflict in school. Also, through interviews and the written report data of student teachers, we were able to gather and use participant-observation notes for analysis. All data were collected, transcribed, and coded to support the identification of themes. The triangulation of data enhanced our ability to identify and clarify patterns while focusing on recurrent themes among the children's constructs of conflict, their reports of conflict behaviors seen in their peers in school, and the conflict behaviors observed by their CRiSP "student-teachers."

The Participants

In each of the three cases, all participants in this study were enrolled in a public middle school in an inner-city environment. Participant ages ranged from twelve to fourteen years of age; two-thirds were female. To maintain the anonymity of the participants in each of the three cases, pseudonyms have been assigned as referents and any characteristic likely to result in the identification of a case has been excluded from this report.

Case Number One: Alpha Middle School

Alpha Middle School (AMS) is located in a modest section of a major southeastern city. Just a few blocks away from the school are tree-lined streets with outdoor cafes, art galleries, trendy coffee shops, and Tudor homes reminiscent of a wealthy southern tradition. CNCR's work with AMS spanned two school years and included forty-eight middle school children, three of whom were Latino, twenty-two of whom were European American, and twenty-three of whom were African American. Of the three cases, the CRiSP-based initiative at AMS was the only "in-school" CRE program where the children received grades for taking the classes; each class had twelve students per semester.

Case Number Two: The Delta After School Program

Through an agreement with the directors of a nonprofit community resource program located in a public housing project, the CRiSP was introduced to children who were enrolled in the Delta After School Program (DASP). Twice a week between nine and twelve African American children would meet in an after-school setting and work with CRiSP student-teachers in a community building adjacent to a Section 8 housing complex. The children were exposed to the same CRE curriculum that was being introduced to children at AMS.

All of the children who attended the DASP lived in the Section 8 housing complex where the program was administered, and all of the children were African American. With the exception of two of the children who were home-schooled, the remainder of the participants attended the same inner-city middle school.

Case Number Three: Omega Middle School

Omega Middle School's (OMS) enrollment is nearly 100 percent African American; thus, like the DASP it was the second virtually monoethnic case in this study. The CRE work conducted with the children of Omega Middle School was also held in an after-school setting. However, unlike the DASP, where the participants were voluntary, the participants in the OMS program were required to attend after-school "detention" sessions for tardiness or other disciplinary problems. Also unlike the DASP, which involved fewer than fifteen children for a two-month period, the OMS program involved approximately fifty children and was conducted five days a week, two hours per day, for two weeks. Consequently, the OMS program was the shortest—yet the most intense—of the three initiatives.

The Student-Teachers

During the course of the study there were two separate groups of approximately thirty student-teachers who worked with the CRiSP as CRE educators and participant-observers. The first group worked extensively with the CNCR director, CNCR staff, and me to prepare to teach CRE to children at Alpha Middle School and the Delta After School Program. The second group of student-teachers worked primarily with me to teach "communications-based" CRE content to children at the Alpha and Omega middle schools. Communications-based CRE content focused on listening, paraphrasing, feedback, verbal, and nonverbal skill enhancement, as opposed to the enhancement of other CR skills related to problem solving, mediation, diversity, and anger management.

The student-teachers assigned to Alpha Middle School were African American, Latino, and European American; those assigned to the Delta After School Program and Omega Middle School were African American. Seventy percent of the student-teachers were female.

The Themes

When the phenomenological constructs and reports of conflict of the Alpha Middle School participants were compared with those of the Delta After School Program participants, and when the student-teacher reports of observed conflict behaviors of the Alpha and Omega Middle School children were compared, three themes emerged suggesting identifiable and shared intragroup conflict orientations and behaviors of the African American children: (1) fears of victimization, (2) identity conflict, and (3) core values.

Fears of Victimization

The first theme that was most associated with the conflict orientations of the African American children involved "fears of victimization." For example, the African American children in the monoethnic DASP case shared explicit concerns related to their expectations of injustice and mistreatment in school settings. One of the children's prominent concerns is "tracking" in educational settings. Yogan (2000) suggests that although tracking is designed to separate students on the basis of intellectual abilities, this practice also separates children according to race, socioeconomics, and other variables. The result is a structural inequality where children incorporate messages about their own inferiority as "more minority and lower income children are placed in low-ability tracks" (Yogan, 2000, p. 112). Accordingly, feedback from the African American children in our study suggests that there are very real—and in some cases legitimate—fears related to being tracked into special education classes as a disciplinary measure. In the words of one young man, "I might get sent to special ed even if I don't have a disability."

The second reference to fear of victimization—"getting jumped"—was expressed frequently by the African American children in the DASP. Getting jumped is a type of bullying behavior where more than one person participates in a physical attack on a single individual. Specifically, the children were concerned about getting jumped (beaten) if they ventured into another school's "zone" (neighborhood). According to the children, one could get jumped by members of a gang or by any group of children who were territorial about having strangers near their school or in their neighborhood.

Identity Conflict

"The topic of black identity has been of genuine concern to psychologists, educators, researchers and social workers for decades. Low self-esteem, self-hatred, and a negative racial identity have been the characteristics traditionally attributed to black children and adults" (Robinson, 2000, p. 5). The most glaring evidence of identity conflict was apparent in the African American children's name-calling behaviors, which were almost exclusively associated with issues of ethnicity, appearance, and intelligence. In fact, these behaviors were consistent in the children's conflict constructs, self-reports of observed conflict, and the student-teacher reports of observed conflict behaviors. For example, in the monoethnic OMS case the children were observed repeatedly calling each other "stupid," "ugly," and "ghetto." One student-teacher reported that the lack of respect associated with the name-calling behaviors was quite apparent and disturbing to her, despite the outbursts of laughter that such behaviors produced among the children. In the monoethnic DASP case, the children reported that name calling was one of the primary reasons for physical confrontation in schools.

A second indication of apparent identity conflict was associated with the African American children's intragroup taunts related to what is often referred to as "colorism." In this case, the children teased each other on the basis of their different shades of skin color. For instance, one child whose skin tone was a very light brown was repeatedly called "white girl" by her classmates. Paradoxically, some of the children taunted others whose skin tones were very dark brown by calling them "black." "The ambivalence about skin color reflects the African American community's ambivalence about identity" (Scott, 2000, p. 23). Name-calling behaviors and taunts associated with colorism were most apparent in the monoethnic settings.

A third pattern of behavior associated with apparent identity conflict involved issues of cultural pride; this was apparent (in contradiction) in both the monoethnic and the multiethnic settings. In the former, the African American children teased each other about trying to "act white" and "talk white"; this teasing occurred most noticeably when their peers responded by using "proper" English to questions posed by the student-teachers. In one case, such taunting resulted in a child's change of verbal expression to incorporate ebonics and slang. On the contrary, in the multiethnic AMS setting, the African American children were observed teasing peers who used ebonics. In the case of the latter, the children called each other "ghetto" and "stupid" for using ebonics in the classroom.

Core Values

Closely related to name calling was the theme of "joning," or verbal warfare; this too was a distinctly prominent behavior among the African American children that occurred primarily in the monoethnic cases. During our focus groups with the children of the DASP, the children reported that joning "happens every day" and is the source of more conflict, including fist fights, than any other social behavior in school. Where the verbal warfare of joning occurs, children take turns volleying criticisms about each other in front of a crowd. The verbal war can often be emotionally brutal and include criticisms of another's appearance, sexual orientation, and family members. It can go on for minutes, hours, days, and even months. In some cases, the joning does not end until the participants engage in physical confrontation.

Joning behavior was most frequently observed during the student-teachers' work with the children in the monoethnic Omega Middle School setting; it was reported as a type of intragroup "cruelty," rife with verbal taunts and relentless teasing among the children. However, there were also reports of joning among the African American children in the multiethnic Alpha Middle School setting. In both cases, the children seemed to value the swift verbal expression ("call and response") skills associated with being able to effectively engage in joning.

In summary, both the reported conflict constructs and observed conflict behaviors of the African American children were primarily related to fears of victimization (tracking and getting jumped), identity conflict (name calling, colorism, and cultural pride), and core values (joning).

Similarities in Adolescent Conflict Orientations: Setting Ethnicity Aside

It is also important to note that there were some similarities among the conflict constructs and behaviors of the children in the three cases, regardless of ethnic distinctions. There were several consistent themes in the self-reports of observed conflict in school. For example, both the AMS and

DASP children reported instances of fighting and gossiping, and the children also indicated that when conflict occurred between boys and girls, school officials consistently disciplined the girls more leniently than the boys. Finally, both groups also referenced conflict between teachers and students as a "normal" occurrence.

In addition to the consistencies found in the children's self-reports of conflicts occurring in school settings, there were also consistencies in the student-teacher reports of observed conflict behaviors that went undifferentiated by ethnicity. For instance, behaviors such as talking over one another, acting out for attention, and fighting or fake fighting were frequently expressed in the student-teacher reports in each of the three cases.

Discussion

The results of this study appear to support the assumption that certain intragroup conflict constructs and behaviors can be associated with shared ethnicity. In our study, there were three apparent distinct conflict themes that emerged among the African American children: fears of victimization, identity conflict, and core values.

One of the fears expressed by the children was that of being placed in a special education classroom even though they were not in need of special education services. In this case, the children referred to specific instances where classmates who misbehaved in the classroom had been mandated to special education classes. In fact, the children seemed to think that there was an impending threat of being placed in a special program as a disciplinary measure more than a true attempt at remedial education. The second most prominent example of a fear of victimization was associated with a type of bullying behavior referred to as getting jumped. In their study on bullying behavior, Jarrett, Davis, Hunt, and Rogers (2000) concluded that "for many young children, schools and neighborhoods are not safe places. Especially in high-poverty neighborhoods, children may be fearful for various reasons" (p. 2). Not surprisingly, children exposed to protracted trauma and threat (such as chronic fears associated with getting jumped) report a higher rate of psychiatric and emotional problems, have greater difficulty developing intellectually, and have a higher incidence of health problems than their nontraumatized peers (Flannery, 1999; Large, 1999). Thus the types of internalized conflicts associated with the children's fears of victimization can manifest themselves in ways that researchers have not even begun to imagine; these fears were most frequently expressed in the monoethnic DASP case.

The second theme or pattern involved conflict constructs and behaviors linked to identity conflict among African American children in both the monoethnic and the multiethnic settings. In this case, intragroup name calling associated with issues of race, intelligence, skin color, and cultural pride appeared to be a source and by-product of identity conflict where essential human needs for recognition, dignity, and safety are threatened (Rothman, 1997).

Pankiw and Bienvenue (1990) observe that "ethnic name calling is not only a violation of human dignity, it is . . . an attack on an individual's identity and can and does have an effect on a person's self-esteem" (p. 78). Certainly, there is pain associated with ethnic name calling, whether it occurs as an intergroup or an intragroup phenomenon. Avrouch (2000) observes that relationships among group members contribute to the negotiation of what can be a positive or negative ethnic identity. Where intragroup name calling occurs, it imposes a latent conflict upon the identity of African American children (Scott, 2000). A sense of ambivalence and angst is created in the mind of a child when another projects upon the child a label (for example, "black") that is undeniably true, yet simultaneously hurtful, and based on often unidentifiable and negative internalizations about oneself; this creates an internal dissonance. When both the name caller and the one who is called the name share the characteristic of the label (for example, a black child calling another black child "black"), the conflict becomes even more perplexing and the dissonance more troubling.

In addition to the issues of name calling and colorism, the issue of cultural pride was also inherent in this theme of identity conflict. One dynamic in particular that appeared to be conflictual for the children involved the use of ebonics. For example, where an African American child's use of ebonics in the monoethnic OMS setting was frequently used as a positive confirmation of African American identity, an African American child's use of ebonics in the multiethnic AMS case was criticized by other African American children. This might indicate the children's presumptions of which contexts are most appropriate or acceptable for using ebonics.

In their survey of the impact of racial and ethnic identity on African American adolescents, Resnicow and others (1999) found that pro-black attitudes were associated with positive attributes such as higher self-esteem, positive behaviors, and positive attitudes about school. This suggests that "having a positive Black identity is a positive attribute" (1999, p. 183). However, as evidenced by our study, the negative issues associated with name calling, colorism, and cultural pride may be so deeply systemic that instilling a positive black identity in children will require measures far beyond, albeit inclusive of, CRE efforts.

The third theme that we discovered involved a difference in cultural values that was most apparent in the joning behavior of the African American children. Joning is closely related to African American verbal traditions such as "playing the dozens," "signifying," and "woofing." According to the website Africana.com, "Social scientists have for years theorized that the dozens is a release for a racially oppressed group, or a way of helping African American males project a masculine identity in a matriarchal culture" (n.d., p. 1). However, in the *Newsletter of the Missouri Center for Safe Schools* (February 1998), the project director proposed that "joning is done for the entertainment of others. The joners are judged by their peers based on how badly they emotionally hurt their victims" (p. 2). This suggests that from a social perspective, the children may value the verbal skills associated with joning (a defensive-offensive conflict escalation device) to a greater degree than they value the verbal skills associated with conflict de-escalation devices.

Implications

As Compton (2000) argues, it is imperative that future CRE research consider the myriad perspectives that race, class, gender, and ethnic differences pose for the field of CRE. In fact, they write, "it is critical that practitioners anticipate [that there will be] differences and identify the norms of target communities prior to designing intervention programs" (Yager and Rotheram-Borus, 2000). Such a targeted approach suggests an appreciation for the values, similarities, and differences of distinct groups.

Future endeavors might also consider more intently how issues of social injustice, oppression, and intragroup conflict have an impact on schoolchildren by affecting intragroup and intergroup relationships. Certainly, any CRE program targeted to children who are members of historically disenfranchised groups should consider these issues, including those that suggest transgenerated trauma such as low self-esteem and self-disdain and so on, prior to program design and implementation.

Researchers should compare and contrast patterns of intragroup and intergroup conflict behaviors to assess the degree to which each affects or provides an impetus for the other; just as an individual's intrapersonal conflicts can affect his or her interpersonal relationships, so too can a group's intrapersonal conflict affect its members' interactions with others. In some instances, it may be necessary to attempt to resolve intragroup conflict issues prior to focusing on intergroup conflict issues.

CRE trainers should be involved in training programs that expand their cultural sensitivity to students' backgrounds, cultural perspectives, and experiential and linguistic backgrounds (Salend and Taylor, 2002), while being equally sensitive to avoid tendencies to stereotype individual students on the basis of group membership. As Gadlin (1994) observes, "Well-intended attempts to associate particular styles or traits with racial or ethnic groups that are, in fact, quite large and diverse can result in stereotyping that is just as distorting and misleading as conventional derogatory stereotyping" (p. 37).

Finally, researchers might consider how the ethnic "climate" of a setting influences or inhibits what may be traditional ethnicity-based conflict orientations or behaviors. For example, it was apparent in our findings that although some of the conflict behaviors exhibited by the African American children in the multiethnic school setting were closely related to those exhibited by the African American children in the monoethnic school setting, the quantity of the behaviors varied. For instance, the children in the monoethnic setting demonstrated far more joning and name calling behaviors and a much greater use of ebonics than did the African American children in the multiethnic setting.

Conclusion

The ethnocentricity of Western dispute resolution philosophy (Gadlin, 1994) continues to dominate many CRE efforts. Beyond this, the propensity to institutionalize "standardized" CRE programs adds to the perpetuation of bias. Accordingly, it is imperative that designers of school-based CRE programs discourage "one-size-fits-all" approaches and instead make serious attempts to incorporate the unique conflict perspectives, orientations, and needs of distinct stakeholder groups into program designs and implementations. To accomplish this, future CRE research initiatives should focus on creating "culturally sensitive functional assessments" (Salend and Taylor, 2002) to incorporate designs that represent all stakeholder groups in a collaborative approach as they develop and implement CRE programs. An action research methodology could be especially supportive of such a collaborative effort since it could broadly assess, reflect, and continuously reassess the needs of the stakeholders instead of imposing values and practices upon them. Clearly, in school settings this type of collaboration could involve the children, parents, teachers, administration, bus drivers, cafeteria workers, and community leaders.

There were certain limitations to this study; therefore its findings should be considered with caution. For example, our cases were restricted to one geographical area, each case was an inner-city public school or school setting, and only one of the programs required participant involvement. It should be noted that CNCR directives stipulated the range of institutions within which research could be conducted; thus the study was affected by additional constraints. The participants selected for this study were chosen primarily because African American adolescents represented the largest number of student participants in the CRiSP CRE initiative during the period of the study. This was not unexpected since the public school system within which the consortium worked reflects a national trend toward increased segregation, with many of the school populations becoming increasingly African American (Brookings Institution, 2000).

As Gadlin notes, "Any effort to describe and take into account cultural differences in dispute resolution, or any other endeavor for that matter, necessarily risks compartmentalizing the phenomenon of racial and gender conflict and separating the psychological dynamics from their social context, which actually heightens discrimination" (1994, p. 38). For this reason, Pankiw and Bienvenue (1990) point to research that "indicates that despite membership in derogated ethnic groups, individual children can still develop a stable, positive self esteem" (p. 81). This perspective is critical to the degree that it will help ward off tendencies to stereotype groups of children on the basis of ethnicity alone, and hopefully it will sensitize researchers to the uniqueness of individuals.

CRE researchers and practitioners can effectively address the conflict needs of diverse groups in society, both children and adults. However, the journey begins when we commit ourselves to the arduous and possibly painful task of working together with those groups to address their specific conflict needs and orientations.

References

Apprey, M. "Reinventing the Self in the Face of Received Transgenerational Hatred in the African American Community." *Mind and Human Interaction*, 1998, *9* (1), 30–37.

Avrouch, K. "Place, Age, and Culture: Community Living and Ethnic Identity Among Lebanese American Adolescents." *Small Group Research,* 2000, *31* (4), 447–470.

Baker, M., French, V., Trujillo, M., and Wing, L. "Impact on Diverse Populations: How CRE Has Not Addressed the Needs of Diverse Populations." In T. S. Jones and D. Kmitta (eds.), *Does It Work? The Case for Conflict Resolution Education in Our Nation's Schools.* Washington, D.C.: Conflict Resolution Education Network, 2000.

Banks, J. "Multicultural Education and the Modification of Students' Racial Attitudes." In W. Hawley and A. Jackson (eds.), *Toward a Common Destiny.* San Francisco: Jossey-Bass, 1995.

Bowland, S. "Reflections on CRE and Diverse Populations." In T. S. Jones and D. Kmitta (eds.), *Does It Work? The Case for Conflict Resolution Education in Our Nation's Schools.* Washington, D.C.: Conflict Resolution Education Network, 2000.

Brookings Institution. "Moving Beyond Sprawl: The Challenge for Metropolitan Atlanta Schools." Washington, D.C. [www.brook.edu/es/urban/atlanta/Schools.htm]. 2000.

Carruthers, W. L., Carruthers, B.J.B., Day-Vines, N. L., Bostick, D., and Watson, D. C. "Conflict Resolution as Curriculum: A Definition, Description and Process for Integration in Core Curricula." *School Counselor,* 1996, *43,* 345–373.

Crawford, D., and Bodine, R. "Conflict Resolution Education: A Guide to Implementing Programs in Schools, Youth-Servicing Organizations and Community Juvenile Justice Settings." Washington, D.C.: Department of Justice, 1996. (ERIC document no. ED 404 426)

Compton, R. "Conflict Resolution Education: Issues of Institutionalization." In T. Jones and D. Kmitta (eds.), *Does It Work? The Case for Conflict Resolution Education in Our Nation's Schools.* Washington, D.C.: Conflict Resolution Education Network, 2000.

Davis, F. *Who Is Black? One Nation's Definition.* University Park: The Pennsylvania State University Press, 1996.

Denzin, N., and Lincoln, Y. *Strategies of Qualitative Inquiry.* Thousand Oaks, Calif.: Sage, 1998.

Flannery, D. "Improving School Violence Prevention Programs Through Meaningful Evaluation." *Choices Briefs.* [http:iume.tc.Columbia.edu/choices/briefs/choices02.html]. 1999.

Gadlin, H. "Conflict Resolution, Cultural Differences and the Culture of Racism." *Negotiation Journal,* 1994, *10* (1), 33–47.

Garfinkel, H. *Studies in Ethnomethodology.* Englewood Cliffs, N.J.: Prentice Hall, 1967.

Georgia Department of Education, Center for Education Policy. *Middle School Report Card.* [doe.k12.ga.us/index.asp]. 2000.

Hairston, C. "African Americans in Mediation Literature: A Neglected Population." *Mediation Quarterly,* 1999, *16* (4), 357–375.

Hall, R. "The Bleaching Syndrome." *Journal of Black Studies,* 1995, *26* (2), 172–185.

Hanish, L. "Children Who Get Victimized at School: What Is Known? What Can Be Done?" *Professional School Counseling,* 2000, *4* (2), 113–120.

"History: The Dozens." [www.africana.com/Articles/]. n.d.

Inger, M. "Conflict Resolution Programs in Schools." Washington, D.C.: Institute of Education Sciences, U.S. Department of Education, 1991. (ERIC document no. ED 338 791)

Jarrett, O., Davis, O., Hunt, M., and Rogers, K. "Fear, Fighting, and Bullying in High-Poverty Environments." Paper presented at the American Educational Research Association Peace SIG Panel, New Orleans, Apr. 24, 2000.

Jones, T., Batton, J., and Carruthers, W. "Conflict Resolution Education: Issues of Institutionalization." In T. Jones and D. Kmitta (eds.), *Does It Work? The Case for Conflict Resolution Education in Our Nation's Schools.* Washington, D.C.: Conflict Resolution Education Network, 2000.

Large, R. "Easing the Strain of Students' Stress." *NEA Today,* 1999, *18* (1), 39.

Lockwood, D. "Violence Among Middle School and High School Students: Analysis and Implications." [www.ncjrs.org/txtfiles/166363.txt]. U.S. Department of Justice, 1997.

Marshall, C., and Rossman, G. *Designing Qualitative Research* (2nd ed.). Thousand Oaks, Calif.: Sage, 1995.

Newsletter of the Missouri Center for Safe Schools. [www.umkc.edu/safeschool/documents/feb98nl.html]. 1998.

Pankiw, B., and Bienvenue, R. "Parental Responses to Ethnic Name Calling: A Sociological Inquiry." *Canadian Ethnic Studies,* 1990, *22* (2), 78–99.

Prothrow-Stith, D. *Deadly Consequences: How Violence Is Destroying Our Teenage Population and a Plan to Begin Solving the Problem.* New York: HarperCollins, 1991.

Ramey, L. "Homicide Among Black Males." *Public Health Reports,* 1980, *95* (6), 549–561.

Resnicow, K., Soler, R., Braithwaite, R., Selassie, M., and Smith, M. "Development of a Racial and Ethnic Identity Scale for African American Adolescents: The Survey of Black Life." *Journal of Black Psychology,* 1999, *25* (2), 171–188.

Robinson, L. "Racial Identity Attitudes and Self-Esteem of Black Adolescents in Residential Care: An Exploratory Study." *British Journal of Social Work,* 2000, *30* (1), 3–25.

Rothman, J. *Resolving Identity Based Conflict in Nations, Organizations and Communities.* San Francisco: Jossey-Bass, 1997.

Salend, S., and Taylor, L. "Cultural Perspectives: Missing Pieces in the Functional Assessment Process." *Intervention in School and Clinic,* 2002, *30* (2), 104–112.

Schutz, A. *On Phenomenology and Social Relations.* Chicago: University of Chicago Press, 1970.

Scott, K. M. "A Perennial Mourning: Identity Conflict and the Transgenerational Transmission of Trauma Within the African American Community." *Mind and Human Interaction,* 2000, *11* (1), 11–26.

Thomas, A. "Impact of Racial Identity on African American Child-Rearing Beliefs." *Journal of Black Psychology,* 2000, *26* (3), 317–330.

Volkan, V. *Blood Lines: From Ethnic Pride to Ethnic Terrorism.* Boulder, Colo.: Westview Press, 1997.

Yager, T., and Rotheram-Borus, M. "Social Expectations Among African-American, Hispanic and European American Adolescents." *Cross-Cultural Research,* 2000, *34* (3), 283–306.

Yogan, L. "School Tracking and Student Violence." *Annals of the Academy of Political and Social Science,* 2000, *567,* 108–123.

K. Michelle Scott is a doctoral candidate in conflict analysis and resolution at Nova Southeastern University and a research fellow at the Consortium on Negotiation and Conflict Resolution.

Building the Container: Curriculum Infusion and Classroom Climate

TRICIA S. JONES
REBECCA SANFORD

This research investigates the impact of conflict resolution education infused into language arts, math, and science curricula on middle school students' perceptions of classroom climate. The pretest, posttest field experiment compared master teachers, novice teachers, and control classes over a yearlong period of intervention. Results give strong evidence for the positive impact of infused conflict education.

Ask a handful of teachers and they will agree that you cannot teach a student who does not feel physically and emotionally safe in class. It is critical to "build the container" of a caring community in the classroom to promote social and emotional development as well as academic achievement. These results from one site in the National Curriculum Integration Project give evidence that CRE builds a caring community.

The National Curriculum Integration Project (NCIP) was initiated in 1996 when a collaborative team of conflict resolution experts committed to developing and piloting a curriculum infusion and integration model for conflict resolution education. The collaborators developed a theoretical model that blended components of conflict resolution education, social and emotional learning, antibias education, and law-related education. In 1998–99, with funding from the Surdna Foundation and the Compton Foundation, they piloted the NCIP program in seven middle schools across the nation (in Louisiana, Maine, Colorado, Massachusetts, Maryland, North Carolina, and California). In 1999, they received funding from the David and Lucile Packard Foundation to conduct and report process evaluation research on that pilot program, and in July 2000 the David and Lucile Packard Foundation provided funding for an out-come evaluation of the NCIP program in four of the original seven middle schools. This article reports on one site in that outcome evaluation research.

NCIP's main goal was to furnish teachers with a process for infusing the critical life skills inherent in conflict resolution education into the for-mal and informal curriculum. Teachers develop ways of addressing several important topics, not as stand-alone issues but woven within the teaching of ongoing curricula (for example, language arts, math, science). The moti-vation for curriculum infusion is the belief that infused conflict education enhances the students' learning environment and chances for academic success (Aber, Brown, and Jones, 2003; Aber and others, 1998).

The NCIP model and program were not standardized across all four sites. Instead, sites were encouraged to develop and implement the pro-gram in a way that met the needs of the school. Thus we report here on one site only, the Colorado site. Our report centers on one of the four research questions in the study: "How does NCIP affect the students' perception of their learning environment in terms of classroom climate and integrated learning process?"

Teachers and administrators know that learning cannot take place unless you nurture a constructive learning environment for students (Brion-Meisels, Rendiero, and Lowenheim, 1984). What is a constructive learning environment? Carol Lieber (2003) defines a constructive learning environ-ment as one in which children feel there is a positive climate and effective classroom management. A constructive learning environment is also a respectful and caring environment where children feel safe to share ideas and feelings.

A constructive, caring classroom community is the foundation for the development of students' social and character development (Elias and others, 1997; Saarni, 1999; Salovey and Sluyter, 1997). Further, enhanced individual competencies promote constructive, prosocial behavior that enacts a caring community (Deutsch, 1973). Deutsch (2000) suggests the most important aspect of constructive sociality is the creation of positive interdependence, or the perception that it is to one's advantage if others do well and it is to one's disadvantage if others do not learn well. Once posi-tive interdependence is established, people are more likely to enact and learn cooperatively, which means less reliance on destructive or competi-tive modes of interaction. Johnson and Johnson (1996) cite several studies that support Deutsch's core theory.

Methodology

The research used a pretest, posttest control group comparison design where the independent variable was teaching condition, with three levels (NCIP returning teachers, NCIP new teachers, and control teachers). The middle school had been involved in the earlier phase for at least two years of training, planning, and implementation. Thus some of the teachers had considerable experience in putting the NCIP principles into practice in their classrooms. Given their experience, the assumption was that the returning NCIP teachers would have the greatest impact on students. Each school also recruited new NCIP teachers for this phase. These teachers had previous information about NCIP but had not received training or participated in the project. Finally, control teachers were selected from volunteers. These teachers did not alter their normal teaching style, had not been exposed to NCIP information, and were unaware of the purpose of NCIP.

Sampling

The Colorado middle school that participated in this project is located in a rural area, has about six hundred students enrolled in seventh, eighth, and ninth grades and has approximately forty teachers and staff. The ethnicity of the student population is 2 percent Native American, 2.4 percent Asian, 1.2 percent African American, 66 percent Caucasian, and 29 percent Hispanic. Approximately 40 percent of the students are on free or reduced rate lunch programs. There is an average 93 percent attendance rate, and a 2 percent dropout rate. Thirteen percent of the student population served out-of-school suspensions for behaviors that created an unsafe environment (fights, gang or gang-related activities, sexual harassment, verbal or physical harassment).

The school has been involved with a number of activities to emphasize constructive conflict resolution and the creation of a safe learning environment. It requires a conflict resolution class (a six-week session) for all seventh graders, and there is a peer mediation program. The school is implementing what is called the Middle Years Program of the International Baccalaureate (MYPIB), which emphasizes five key areas of performance to be woven throughout all academic and nonacademic school activities. The Middle Years Program was developed in the 1999–2000 school year and was piloted in the seventh grade in the 2000–01 school year. The areas of concern in this program overlap with some of the key topic areas of NCIP.

Classes for data collection were selected using three criteria. First, classes had to be yearlong, with the same students participating in the entire academic year from September through June. Second, NCIP and control classes had to be from the same grade levels. Although there were ninth-grade classes that volunteered to act as control classes, there were no ninth-grade NCIP classes, so all data were collected from seventh and eighth grades. The third criterion was the willingness of the teacher.

Two hundred sixty-three questionnaires were collected from the NCIP classes (141 from returning NCIP classes and 122 from new NCIP classes), and 241 questionnaires were collected from control classes. In terms of student gender, 286 responses were from males, 187 responses were from females, and 31 students did not indicate gender. In terms of grade level, 183 questionnaires were from the seventh grade and 321 were from the eighth grade. In terms of class subject matter, 166 questionnaires were from English classes, 35 were from math classes, 153 were from science classes, and 150 were from other classes (history and geography). One hundred seventy-nine questionnaires were gathered in the pretest, 172 in posttest one, and 153 in posttest two.

Measurement

Two sources of data helped answer the research question: the Classroom Life Survey and student focus group interviews.

Classroom Life Survey (CLS)

The CLS instrument is derived from the long form of the Classroom Life Measure (CLM), developed and validated by David and Roger Johnson. However, the full CLM was not used in this research for two reasons. First, it is a ninety-item measure designed to assess middle school students' perceptions of their classroom climate. In previous testing, we found the length of the questionnaire caused serious fatigue for students and made it difficult to complete data collection within one class period. In addition, the long version of the CLM was designed to measure an entire collaborative learning environment. Our project was not based on collaborative learning procedures, making much of the measure irrelevant for our uses.

We shortened the measure and added items to include dimensions relevant to NCIP goals. The result was the Classroom Life Survey (CLS), a twenty-four-item survey measuring five factors: safety, student support, teacher support, cohesion, and constructive conflict management. In addition, we calculated an overall climate score by summing across all items on the measure. For each item, students are asked to respond in terms of the specific class they are in. Response options are that the statement is "completely false," "false much of the time," "sometimes true and sometimes false," "true much of the time," or "completely true." For copies of the measure, consult Jones, Sanford, and Bodtker (2001).

Reliability was assessed for the Classroom Life Survey measure. Cronbach's alpha for the overall Classroom Life Measure was .88. However, the reliability on the individual subscales was problematic in certain cases, and some items were deleted from subscales to improve reliability prior to further analysis. The safety subscale (which originally comprised items two, six, nineteen, twenty, and twenty-four) had two items removed (items two and twenty) to increase the reliability to a marginally acceptable .65; the two items removed both referred to perceptions of physical safety in the school and classroom. The remaining items dealt with perceptions of psychological and emotional safety. The student support subscale had an internal consistency of .80. The teacher support subscale had an alpha of .79. The constructive conflict management subscale had a marginally acceptable reliability of .64 after item seventeen was dropped. It dealt with whether the teacher determined who was right during disputes. The cohesion subscale was able to attain only a .57 reliability even after item four was dropped; it referred to a student's perception that she or he should get along with other students in the class better than she or he does.

Student Focus Groups

Student focus group interviews were conducted in both posttest periods. In February 2001, three student focus groups were held. All of these interviews occurred during the students' lunch periods. In May 2001, two student focus group interviews were held. Students were asked to participate in the interviews while their classmates were completing the final questionnaire administration.

Program Implementation

Participating teachers were trained in two two-day sessions concentrating on the key conflict skills and classroom practices discussed later in this article. Teachers agreed to focus on implementing the curriculum infusion daily. The specific lessons and techniques used were monitored by activity logs to ensure program implementation fidelity.

The critical conflict resolution skills taught to students were active/ reflective listening, affirmation, anger management, brainstorming/ integrative thinking, giving and receiving feedback, identifying feelings, *I* messages/assertiveness, managing emotions, interrupting prejudice/ bias, perspective taking, problem solving/relationship building, and working cooperatively. The classroom practices that were taught to teachers and emphasized in this NCIP program implementation were class guidelines/constitution, collaborative decision making, dialogue versus debate/constructive controversy, energizers/teambuilders, gatherings/closings, morning meetings, negotiating, sharing circles, and win-win discipline.

The site coordinator used a tutorial model that had served this school well in the first years of involvement with NCIP. This model focused on one-on-one meetings between the site coordinator and each NCIP teacher. Approximately every two weeks the site coordinator met with an NCIP to observe classroom technique, review lesson plans and integrated units being developed, and to teach new exercises and approaches.

Data Analysis

The quantitative questionnaire data were analyzed using two-way ANOVAs (test time by teaching condition). In some cases, the teaching condition variable was analyzed in terms of all three possible levels: returning NCIP classes, new NCIP classes, and control classes. However, in some cases (where review of initial descriptive data indicated) only two levels of the teaching condition variable were used (NCIP versus control). All statistical analyses were performed using the SPSSXPC software program.

Data from site coordinator, student, and teacher interviews were transcribed and analyzed for dominant themes. Activity logs and integrated lesson plan documents furnished by teachers were used as supplementary data to explain in more detail the nature of the program implementation. For further information on integrated lessons developed and implemented in the NCIP project, see www.ncip.org.

Results

The results of the three-way ANOVAs (test time by teaching condition by student gender) on the classroom climate variables (the overall classroom climate score and each of the subscale scores for cohesion, student support, teacher support, constructive conflict management, and safety) suggests that the NCIP experience had a significant impact on students' perceptions of their learning environment. The expectation was that over the academic year the returning NCIP classes should show a more positive classroom climate than the new NCIP classes and both NCIP conditions should have a more positive classroom climate than the control classes. The results strongly support this expectation.

Classroom Life Measure

There was a significant test time by teaching condition interaction effect (F = 3.46, df = 4/417, p < .01, eta = .032) for the overall climate variable. The graph of means presented in Figure 1 shows that the returning NCIP classes developed increasingly more positive climate, from the pretest (mean = 3.46, sd = .53) to the first posttest (mean = 3.66, sd = .49) and to the last posttest (mean = 3.79, sd = .48). New NCIP classes showed an initial increase in overall climate from the pretest (mean = 3.21, sd = .43) to the first posttest period (mean = 3.52, sd = .58), but there was a plateau in perceptions of classroom climate at this level, not substantially increasing for the last posttest (mean = 3.49, sd = .48). Conversely, the control classes showed a slight but steady decrease in perceptions of classroom climate from the pretest (mean = 3.21, sd = .43) through the first posttest (mean = 3.15, sd = .50) and second posttest (mean = 3.10, sd = .55).

Figure 1. Graph of NCIP Condition for Overall Climate

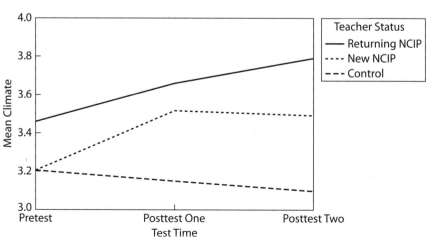

A similar pattern was found for the significant test time by teaching condition interaction effect for the student support subscale (F = 3.45, df = 4/417, p < .01, eta = .032). This subscale measures the extent to which students feel they are liked and accepted by the other students in the class. Figure 2 shows the graph of this interaction. Again, there is a significant and sustained increase in perceptions of student support for the returning NCIP classes (pretest mean = 3.16, sd = .83; posttest one mean = 3.38, sd = .72; posttest two mean = 3.55, sd = .71). New NCIP classes showed a strong initial increase followed by a plateau, but they did not decrease (pretest mean = 2.78, sd = .75; posttest one mean = 3.21, sd = .82; posttest two mean = 3.18, sd = .71). Further, control classes showed a slight decrease in perceived student support over the academic year (pretest mean = 2.99, sd = .83; posttest one mean = 2.82, sd = .79; posttest two mean = 2.86, sd = .82).

The test time by teaching condition interaction effect for the teacher support subscale approached significance (F = 1.91, df = 4/417, p < .10, eta = .018). The teacher support subscale measured the extent to which students felt the teacher cared for them, and cared about them personally, as well as their academic progress. Figure 3 shows that returning NCIP classes showed continuous increases in perceived teacher support (pretest mean = 4.08, sd = .85; posttest one mean = 4.19, sd = .82; posttest two mean = 4.28, sd = .85), but new NCIP classes showed a very small initial increase that soon fell below original levels (pretest

Figure 2. Graph of NCIP Condition for Student Support Dimension

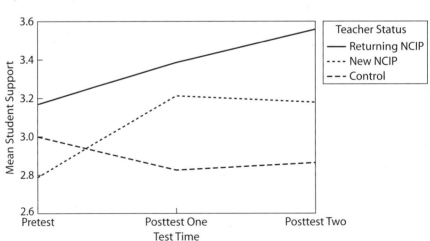

Figure 3. Graph of NCIP Condition for Teacher Support Dimension

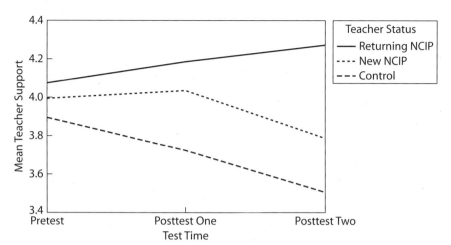

mean = 4.00, sd = .66; posttest one mean = 4.04, sd = .83; posttest two mean = 3.80, sd = .87). Control classes showed a steady decrease of perceived teacher support throughout the year (pretest mean = 3.90, sd = .88; posttest one mean = 3.73, sd = .95; posttest two mean = 3.52, sd = 1.07).

The test time by teaching condition interaction effect for the cohesion subscale was also significant (F = 2.48, df = 4/417, $p < .05$, eta = .023). The cohesion subscale measured the extent to which students felt that the class had cohered into a supportive group or community. As Figure 4 shows, the returning NCIP classes showed a strong initial increase in perceived cohesion that was sustained during the posttest periods (pretest mean = 3.58, sd = .71; posttest one mean = 3.85, sd = .72; posttest two mean = 3.89, sd = .69). New NCIP classes had an initial increase, and again the increase was sustained over the posttest period (pretest mean = 3.20, sd = .67; posttest one mean = 3.61, sd = .71; posttest two mean = 3.70, sd = .55); however, the pretest levels of perceived cohesion were significantly lower for new NCIP classes than returning NCIP classes. Control classes demonstrated no change from pretest through posttests (pretest mean = 3.22, sd = .77; posttest one mean = 3.22, sd = .68; posttest two mean = 3.17, sd = .78).

Although the results for the constructive conflict management and safety subscales were not significant in terms of interaction effects comparing all three levels of teaching condition across test times, the data seemed

Figure 4. Graph of NCIP Condition for Cohesion

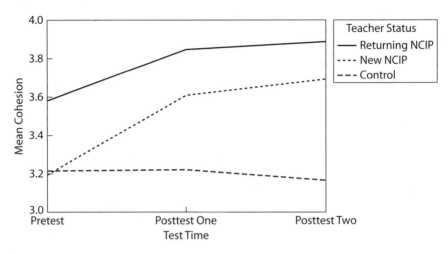

to suggest that there may be significant differences when all NCIP classes were compared with control classes. So a two-way ANOVA was run looking mainly at interaction effects for two teaching conditions (NCIP versus control) across the three test times (pretest, posttest one, posttest two). The ANOVAs revealed significant interaction effects for both the constructive conflict management subscale ($F = 3.12$, df $= 2/423$, $p < .05$, eta $= .014$) and the safety subscales ($F = 3.46$, df $= 2/423$, $p < .05$, eta $= .016$). The constructive conflict management subscale measured students' perceptions that conflicts in class were constructively managed and students were empowered to solve their own conflicts. The safety subscale measured the students' perceptions that they felt physically and psychologically safe in the class. In both cases, NCIP classes showed significant increases across the academic year while control classes showed slight decreases (constructive conflict management NCIP pretest mean $= 3.00$, sd $= .67$; posttest one mean $= 3.15$, sd $= .58$; posttest two mean $= 3.25$, sd $= .67$; control class pretest mean $= 2.84$, sd $= .63$; posttest one mean $= 2.79$, sd $= .62$; posttest two mean $= 2.72$, sd $= .69$). (Safety NCIP pretest mean $= 3.27$, sd $= .82$; posttest one mean $= 3.58$, sd $= .85$; posttest two mean $= 3.66$, sd $= .80$; control class pretest mean $= 2.84$, sd $= .67$; posttest one mean $= 2.86$, sd $= .93$; posttest two mean $= 2.79$, sd $= .84$.)

Of course, there were also significant main effects for the teaching condition variable for all of the classroom climate variables. Ordinarily these main effects would not be reported, but they are mentioned here largely because of the relatively healthy effect sizes associated with these main effects. All of these effects were significant at the $p < .001$ level at 2/417 degrees of freedom. The F tests and their effect size were overall climate $F = 40.29$, eta $= .161$; constructive conflict management $F = 21.65$, eta $= .094$; cohesion $F = 21.48$, eta $= .093$; safety $F = 41.39$, eta $= .165$; student support $F = 15.11$, eta $= .067$; teacher support $F = 14.88$, eta $= .066$). In all cases, returning NCIP teachers had significantly higher scores on these measures than new NCIP teachers, who in turn had significantly higher scores than control teachers.

Student Interviews

Listening to the students made it obvious that they perceived an important difference in the learning environment in the NCIP classes and their other classes. Here is a summary of the major points that came from the thematic analyses of their interviews.

Group-Based Learning. The students commented that they appreciated the ability to engage in group-based learning for many of their projects. They noted that this learning structure resulted in more time to interact with other students, less formal lecture presentation, and more responsibility for learning the material themselves.

Life-Relevant Projects. It was evident that many of the projects in the NCIP classes struck a chord with students. They felt the projects were truly relevant to their life situations and helped them to understand themselves and their orientation to social issues.

Sustained and Integrated Projects. Several of the students commented that they were able to learn much more and learn better because the units of learning were sustained over a fairly long period of time (three to six weeks) and required them to integrate traditional learning approaches with novel reflective approaches.

Teacher Demonstrates Respect for Students. In terms of student-teacher relationships, students had more to say about mutual respect than any other factor. They often noted how important it was to them that NCIP teachers treated them with respect and expected them to treat others with respect. Some students commented that NCIP teachers were more willing to negotiate with students but also held students to a high standard of behavior. In essence, the NCIP teachers modeled for students how to be respectful and create a positive relationship with others.

Teacher Caring. Students felt that NCIP teachers cared more for them and about them than did other teachers they had. Several commented that their NCIP teachers seemed to know more about their lives and were more in touch with things that affected their school work and attitude.

Emphasis on Ability to Work with Others. These feelings were strongly linked to the group work. Students noted that they learned more about how to work with others and how to communicate with others in the NCIP classes. Part of this was necessity; since group projects had shared grades, they had to learn to work together if they were to succeed. But part of this was simply the ability to learn to express themselves with others and to understand what others intended and wanted.

Emphasis on Need to Respect Others. Many students commented that the NCIP classes reinforced some of the skills for respecting others that they learned in the seventh-grade conflict management class, where students are taught to be in the moment, use appropriate body language, use appropriate eye contact, give appropriate feedback, and ask questions to clarify or validate the other.

Emphasis on Need to Handle Conflicts Constructively. When students have to work together to succeed, they learn the importance of being able to handle conflict constructively. Students noted that a big difference between the NCIP teachers and their other teachers was that the latter immediately intervened to handle a conflict between students rather than give students a chance to handle it themselves. NCIP teachers were far more patient but let students know that they would be there if needed.

Implications for Practice

The NCIP data leave no doubt that conflict resolution education infused into ongoing curricula can have a significant and lasting impact on classroom climate. Students feel they have much more support from other students, both personally and academically. They perceive more support and interest from their teachers, and feel more respected by their teachers. Students perceive a stronger sense of community, which carries over to a variety of orientations to learning in the classroom (such as service-based learning, group and cooperative learning).

Knowing the benefits of CRE curriculum infusion answers the question of whether or not doing it encourages more careful consideration of *how* to do it. Process evaluation in the Colorado NCIP site offered insights in the areas of training, planning, teacher team development, and outside site support. Training should closely model content and approaches teachers are expected to use in their classes. The more that training can demonstrate the essential skills and practices and give teachers an opportunity to begin using them, the better prepared they are. Like their students, teachers need skill development and direct instruction that emphasizes learning patterns with repetition and reinforcement (Adalbjarnardottir and Selman, 1997). Rachel Poliner (2003) talks about the learning curve needed for students and teachers to learn new skills. Knowledge is only the first step. Without practice, application, and review, the new skill will not really be learned. Her discussion of curriculum infusion programs underscores how patient we need to be when asking teachers to develop new teaching skills.

Planning and goal setting among teachers is imperative. In the initial training session, NCIP teachers were encouraged to set goals for themselves and to reflect on how the NCIP goals would mesh with the international baccalaureate goals. This was an important aspect of the success of the project. It enabled the teachers to see these goals as parallel and supportive, rather than competitive processes. Moreover, it helped teachers to think in terms of specific assessment practices that they could use to monitor their teaching progress and their students' progress during the year. Team development was still hampered significantly by an absence of meeting time for the full NCIP teaching team. The NCIP teachers were able to overcome this in two ways. First, the senior or returning NCIP teachers were helpful to new NCIP teachers, offering lesson examples, advice, and general support. The returning NCIP teachers were able to model teaching practices that the new NCIP teachers could use. The second way the team was able to overcome the lack of team meeting time was the use of the tutorial process with the site coordinator.

One of the tensions experienced in NCIP was the need for readily available integrated lessons (especially for novice teachers) and the advantages of creating your own integrated lessons. It is difficult for teachers to find the time to develop an entire infused curriculum of integrated CRE lessons and units. Therefore building on the previous work of others is helpful. The more sophisticated teachers become, the more their integrated units have the power to transform students and learning environments.

Excellent examples of integrated lessons are available from the School Mediation Center, the Ohio Commission on Dispute Resolution and Conflict Management, and the Colorado Department of Education, as well as other organizations.

Implications for Research

A number of directions need to be explored. The link between curriculum-infused CRE, climate, and academic achievement, already initially explored by Stevahn and her colleagues (Stevahn, 2000), deserves further examination. Especially with "teach to the test" pressures, it is important to demonstrate that creating a safe learning environment through CRE means creating a more effective learning environment in terms of academic achievement indices (Sandy and Cochran, 2000).

We desperately need research that turns the focus on benefits for teachers as well as students (Kmitta and others, 2000). One of the most significant challenges of our education system is an alarming rate of teacher attrition; national statistics indicate that the average length of stay in the profession for a new teacher is three years (National Center for Educational Statistics, 2000). A poor teacher retention rate may be due to teachers feeling overwhelmed and underprepared to manage classes and create learning environments that are necessary in order to teach content. CRE curriculum infusion could be quite helpful in addressing these concerns and in encouraging teachers to remain in schools that are in greatest need of their influence. CRE infusion could also help with the creation of an overall safe school environment that would, in turn, encourage teacher development (King, Wagner, and Hedrick, 2001).

As always, we need more longitudinal research on this as well as other CRE issues. What are the long-term benefits for students, teachers, and schools that are presented the opportunity to learn these skills and create caring and constructive learning environments?

References

Aber, J. L., Brown, J. I., and Jones, S. M. "Developmental Trajectories Toward Violence in Middle Childhood: Course, Demographic Differences, and Response to School-Based Intervention." *Developmental Psychology,* 2003, *39* (2), 324–348.

Aber, J. L., Jones, S. M., Brown, J. L., Chaudry, N., and Samples, F. "Resolving Conflict Creatively: Evaluating the Developmental Effects of a School-Based

Violence Prevention Program in Neighborhood and Classroom Context." *Development and Psychopathology,* 1998, *10* (2), 187–213.

Adalbjarnardottir, S., and Selman, R. "'I Feel I Have Received a New Vision': An Analysis of Teachers' Professional Development as They Work with Students on Interpersonal Issues." *Teaching and Teacher Education,* 1997, *13,* 409–428.

Brion-Meisels, S., Rendiero, B., and Lowenheim, G. "Student Decision Making: Improving School Climate for All Students." In S. Braaten, R. Rutherford, Jr., and C. Kardash (eds.), *Programming for Adolescents with Behavioral Disorders.* Reston, Va.: Council for Exceptional Children, 1984.

Deutsch, M. *The Resolution of Conflict: Constructive and Destructive Processes.* New Haven, Conn.: Yale University Press, 1973.

Deutsch, M. "Cooperation and Competition." In M. Deutsch and P. Coleman (eds.), *Handbook of Conflict Resolution.* San Francisco: Jossey-Bass, 2000.

Elias, M. J., Zins, J. E., Weissberg, R. P., Frey, K. S., Greenberg, M. T., Haynes, N. M., Kessler, R., Shwab-Stone, M. E., and Shriver, T. P. (eds.). *Promoting Social and Emotional Learning: Guidelines for Educators.* Alexandria, Va.: Association for Supervision and Curriculum Development, 1997.

Johnson, D. W., and Johnson, R. T. "Conflict Resolution and Peer Mediation Programs in Elementary and Secondary Schools: A Review of the Research." *Review of Educational Research,* 1996, *66,* 459–506.

Jones, T. S., Sanford, R., and Bodtker, A. *The National Curriculum Integration Project: Research Report.* Philadelphia: Temple University College of Allied Health Professions, 2001.

King, K. A., Wagner, D., and Hedrick, B. "Safe and Drug Free: Coordinators' Perceived Needs to Improve Violence and Drug Prevention Programs." *Journal of School Health,* 2001, *71* (6), 236–242.

Kmitta, D., Brown, J., Chappell, C., Spiegler, J., and Wiley, P. "Impact on Educators: Conflict Resolution Education and the Evidence Regarding Educators." In T. S. Jones and D. Kmitta (eds.), *Does It Work? The Case for Conflict Resolution Education in Our Nation's Schools.* Washington, D.C.: Association for Conflict Resolution, 2000.

Lieber, C. M. "The Building Blocks of Conflict Resolution Education: Direct Instruction, Adult Modeling, and Core Practices." In T. S. Jones and R. Compton (eds.), *Kids Working It Out: Stories and Strategies for Making Peace in Our Schools.* San Francisco: Jossey-Bass, 2003.

National Center for Educational Statistics. Washington, D.C.: U.S. Government Printing Office, 2000.

Poliner, R. "Making Meaningful Connections: Curriculum Infusion." In T. S. Jones and R. Compton (eds.), *Kids Working It Out: Stories and Strategies for Making Peace in Our Schools.* San Francisco: Jossey-Bass, 2003.

Saarni, C. *The Development of Emotional Competence.* New York: Guilford Press, 1999.

Salovey, P., and Sluyter, D. (eds.). *Emotional Development and Emotional Intelligence: Educational Implications.* New York: Basic Books, 1997.

Sandy, S. V., and Cochran, K. M. "The Development of Conflict Resolution Skills in Children: Preschool to Adolescence." In M. Deutsch and P. Coleman (eds.), *Handbook of Conflict Resolution.* San Francisco: Jossey-Bass, 2000.

Stevahn, L. "School Conflict Programs and Climate: What Matters and Why." In T. S. Jones and D. Kmitta (eds.), *Does It Work? The Case for Conflict Resolution Education in Our Nation's Schools.* Washington, D.C.: Association for Conflict Resolution, 2000.

Tricia S. Jones is a professor in the Department of Psychological Studies at Temple University in Philadelphia.

Rebecca Sanford is an instructor in the Department of Speech Communication at Monmouth State University in Monmouth, New Jersey.

Cost-Benefit Analysis of CRE Programs in Ohio

JENNIFER BATTON

This article describes the findings from a preliminary cost-benefit analysis of the Ohio School Conflict Management Initiative, the second phase of the OSCMI evaluation, for "at its most useful, benefit-cost analysis can identify and provide information on the full costs of programs and weigh those against the dollar value of the program benefits" (Kee, 1994, p. 456).

There were seventy-one schools in Ohio receiving training in conflict management for school year 2002–03. In those schools, there were 41,282 students. The Ohio Commission on Dispute Resolution and Conflict Management's reported budget is approximately $600,000 for fiscal year 2003. Dividing the budget by the number of students and schools across the state of Ohio yields an average cost per student of $14.53 and per school of $8,450.70. These are liberal estimates of the cost of the OSCMI. There are a number of other schools that use the commission's resources during the year that were intentionally not included in the cost estimate because of the difficulty of linking their benefits to the resources they consume. This number also does not take into consideration that the $600,000 also goes toward salary for a fiscal administrator at ODE (Ohio Department of Education), administrative costs at ODE, and a number of other trainings and workshops for higher education and pre-K–12 schools that are not included in the study. On the basis of this information, the cost ratio is actually greater than the actual cost per school.

NOTE: *The Bureau of Research Training and Services (BRTS) at Kent State University, under the leadership of Ray Hart, evaluated the impact of the Ohio School Conflict Management Initiative (OSCMI) grant.*

Disciplinary Cost Details

Detentions are held after school twice a week for a half hour per session. A teacher needs to be hired to monitor the detention each time it is held. In a thirty-six-week school year, at twice a week for 0.5 hours each, there will be a maximum of thirty-six hours of detention that need to be monitored. A teacher is then hired at $25.10 an hour for thirty-six hours; it will then cost a school $903.60 per year to hold detentions after school. This total does not include the time needed to handle a student disruption and administer a detention ($32.40 each); several students may attend a detention at the same time. The same process applies for hiring teacher monitors for Saturday schools and in-school suspensions. A Saturday school occurs for three hours once a week for a thirty-six-week school year, which totals $2,710.80. A teacher hired for an in-school suspension monitoring would work eight hours a day, five days a week, for thirty-six weeks. The in-school suspension hiring will cost $36,144.00. The discipline data reported through EMIS on the ODE website lists for one year at each school the student enrollment, total disciplines, expulsions, withdrawals for expulsion, out-of-school suspensions, and all other disciplines.

The Grant Recipient Schools

When focusing on the seventy-one schools receiving conflict management training this school year, one finds an average of 581 students per school, which costs $8,441.93 per school to fund the OSCMI program. On average, there are 128 reported disciplines a year per school. The number of students actually disciplined cannot be determined, and only percentages of the total population are reported. From the seventy-one schools in conflict management, each school typically has one expulsion, fifty-two out-of-school suspensions, and seventy-five other disciplines per year. The "other disciplines" category is composed of in-school suspensions, Saturday schools, and any additional but not otherwise specified disciplines.

Because it is impossible to determine the number of detentions, Saturday schools, and in-school suspensions administered for each school, no firm estimate of cost for the other-disciplines category can be applied and subsequently compared to the cost for implementing the OSCMI program. The only costs that may be computed per school for disciplinary actions are expulsions and out-of-school suspensions. A school will spend $431.40 per expulsion and $12,006.80 on fifty-two out-of-school suspensions, which equals $12,437.20. This cost is already more than what it costs to implement the conflict management program one time ($8,441.43), and a school will also spend that amount on discipline issues every year. The yearly costs for hiring monitors for detentions, Saturday schools, and in-school suspensions, as noted earlier, equals $39,758.40. The total calculated cost for discipline issues now equates to $52,195.60 for each school per year; this total does not yet include the additional cost for the seventy-five other disciplines.

Reference

Kee, J. E. "Benefit-Cost Analysis in Program Evaluation." In J. Wholey, H. P. Hatry, and K. E. Newcomer (eds.), *Handbook of Practical Program Evaluation.* San Francisco: Jossey-Bass, 1994.

Jennifer Batton is director of the schools programs at the Ohio Commission for Dispute Resolution and Conflict Management.

INFORMATION FOR CONTRIBUTORS

Conflict Resolution Quarterly publishes scholarship on relationships between theory, research, and practice in the conflict management and dispute resolution field to promote more effective professional applications. *Conflict Resolution Quarterly* is sponsored by the Association for Conflict Resolution (formerly the Academy of Family Mediators, the Society for Professionals in Dispute Resolution and the Conflict Resolution Education Network).

Articles may focus on any aspect of the conflict resolution process or context, but a primary focus is the behavior, role, and impact of third parties in effectively handling conflict. All theoretical and methodological orientations are welcome. Submission of scholarship with the following emphases is encouraged:

- Discussion of a variety of third-party conflict resolution practices, including dialogue, facilitation, facilitated negotiation, mediation, fact-finding, and arbitration

- Analyses of disputant and third-party behavior, preference, and reaction to conflict situations and conflict management processes

- Consideration of conflict processes in a variety of conflict contexts, including family, organizational, community, court, health care, commercial, international, and educational contexts

- Sensitivity to relational, social, and cultural contexts that define and impact conflict

- Interdisciplinary analyses of conflict resolution and scholarship providing insights applicable across conflict resolution contexts

- Discussion of conflict resolution training and education processes, program development, and program evaluation and impact for programs focusing on the development of more competent conflict resolution in educational, organizational, community, or professional contexts

A defining focus of the journal is the relationships among theory, research, and practice. All articles should specifically address the implications of theory for practice and research directions, how research can better inform practice, or how research can contribute to theory development with important implications for practice.

Conflict Resolution Quarterly publishes conventional articles and other features, including the following:

- *State-of-the-art articles:* Articles providing a comprehensive reporting of current literature on a specific topic and a critique of that theory and research in terms of how well it informs conflict practice.
- *Implications-for-practice commentary:* Readers' comments on the implications for practice of previously published articles, discussing how the articles have informed them in terms of practice.
- *Book reviews:* Reviews of current books on conflict management and dispute resolution. Preference is given to book review essays that review three or more books in a related topic area in light of current scholarship in that area.
- *Training and education notes:* Short articles focusing on the practice of dispute resolution training, studies of dispute resolution training, or reviews of curricula or software programs for dispute resolution training.

Manuscript Preparation

All submissions should be prepared according to the *Chicago Manual of Style* (14th edition, University of Chicago Press). Double-space everything in the manuscript, including quotes and references. Indent the first line of each paragraph and leave no extra space between paragraphs. Margins should be at least one inch wide, and there should be no more than 250 words per manuscript page. Use 8½-inch × 11-inch nonerasable bond paper and type or print on one side only. The printed copy from word processors must be in regular typewriter face, not dot matrix type.

The text should be directed to a multidisciplinary audience and be as readable and practical as possible. Illustrate theoretical ideas with specific examples, explain technical terms in nontechnical language, and keep the style clear. Do not include graphs or statistical tables unless necessary for clarity. Spell out such abbreviations as *e.g., etc., i.e., et al.,* and *vs.* in their English equivalents—in other words, use *for example, and so on, that is, and others,* and *versus* (except in legal cases, where *v.* is used).

Conventional Articles and State-of-the-Art Articles. These papers should be no longer than thirty double-spaced pages of text (or 7,500 words). Submissions should include a cover page providing title and author name(s) and contact information (address, telephone number, and e-mail address). Submissions should also include a short abstract of the article (no more than 100 words). Hard-copy paper submissions should include three copies of the paper with a detachable cover page.

Practitioner Responses, Implications-for-Practice, Commentary, Book Reviews, and Training and Education Notes. These features should be no more than ten double-spaced pages of text (or 2,500 words). Submissions should contain a cover page clearly indicating the nature of the submission and providing author name(s) and contact information. Papers can be submitted via e-mail if sent as a file attachment prepared in Word 6.0 or 7.0 or in rich text format. Hard-copy paper submissions should include three copies of the paper with a detachable cover page.

Citations and References. Cite all sources of quotations or attributed ideas in the text, including the original page number of each direct quotation and statistic, according to the following examples:

Knight (1983) argues cogently that references are a pain in the neck. As one authority states, "References are a pain in the neck" (Knight, 1983, p. 35).

Do not use footnotes. Incorporate all footnote material into the text proper, perhaps within parentheses. (Brief *endnotes,* if used sparingly, are acceptable and should be double-spaced in numerical order and placed before the reference section. Endnotes must not contain bibliographical data.)

Use the following examples in typing references:

Single-author book or pamphlet
Hunter, J. E. *Meta-Analysis: Cumulating Research Findings Across Studies.* Newbury Park, Calif.: Sage, 1982.

Multiple-author book or pamphlet
Hammond, D. C., Hepworth, D. H., and Smith, V. G. *Improving Therapeutic Communication: A Guide for Developing Effective Techniques.* San Francisco: Jossey-Bass, 1977.

Edited book/multiple edition
Brakel, S. J., and Rock, R. S. (eds.). *The Mentally Disabled and the Law.* (2nd ed.) Chicago: University of Chicago Press, 1971.

Chapter in an edited book
Patterson, G. R. "Beyond Technology: The Next Stage in the Development of Parent Training." In L. L'Abate (ed.), *Handbook of Family Psychology and Therapy.* Vol. 2. Homewood, Ill.: Dorsey Press, 1985.

Journal or magazine article
Aussieker, B., and Garabino, J. W. "Measuring Faculty Unionism: Quantity and Quality." *Industrial Relations,* 1973, *12* (1), 117–124.

Paper read at a meeting
Sherman, L. W., Gartin, P. R., Doi, D., and Miler, S. "The Effects of Jail Time on Drunk Drivers." Paper presented at the American Society of Criminology, Atlanta, Nov. 6, 1986.

Unpublished report
Keim, S. T., and Carney, M. K. "A Cost-Benefit Study of Selected Clinical Education Programs for Professional and Allied Health Personnel." Arlington, Va.: Bureau of Business and Economic Research, University of Texas, 1975.

Government report
Florida Advisory Council on Intergovernmental Relations. *Impact Fees in Florida.* Tallahassee: Florida Advisory Council on Intergovernmental Relations, 1986.

Unpublished dissertation
Johnson, W. P. "A Study of the Acceptance of Management Performance Evaluation Recommendations by Federal Agencies: Lessons from GAO Reports Issued in FY 1983." Unpublished doctoral dissertation, Department of Business Administration, George Mason University, Washington, D.C., 1986.

Figures, Tables, and Exhibits. Clean copies of figures should accompany the manuscript. Upon an article's acceptance, authors must provide camera-ready artwork. Tables, figures, and exhibits should be double-spaced on separate pages, and table notes should be keyed to the body of the table with letters rather than with numbers or asterisks. Exhibits (used in place of appendixes) should also be typed double-spaced on separate pages. All figures, tables, and exhibits should have short, descriptive titles and must be called out in the text.

Publication Process

When a manuscript is accepted for publication, authors are asked to sign a letter of agreement granting the publisher the right to copyedit, publish, and copyright the material. Manuscripts under review for possible publication in *Conflict Resolution Quarterly* should not be submitted for review elsewhere or have been previously published elsewhere.

Article submissions and questions regarding editorial matters should be sent to:

Tricia S. Jones, Editor
Conflict Resolution Quarterly
Department of Psychological Studies
College of Education
Temple University
Philadelphia, PA 19122
tsjones@astro.temple.edu

ORDERING INFORMATION